Laughter the Best Medicine

Laughter the Best Medicine

The Funniest Jokes, Stories and Cartoons from *Reader's Digest*

Reader's Digest
New York/Montreal

Chief Content Officer, Reader's Digest Jason Buhrmester
Content Director Mark Hagen
Creative Director Raeann Thompson
Senior Editor Julie Kuczynski
Editors Christine Campbell, Sara Strauss
Associate Creative Director Kristen Stecklein
Deputy Editor, Copy Desk Dulcie Shoener
Copy Editor Elizabeth Pollock Bruch
Contributing Designer Jennifer Tokarski

A READER'S DIGEST BOOK

485 Lexington Avenue
New York, NY 10017

Cover photo: smrm1977/Getty Images

ISBN 978-1-62145-998-9 (dated)
ISBN 978-1-62145-999-6 (undated)

Component number:
119300112S (dated)
119300114S (undated)

Printed in China
1 3 5 7 9 10 8 6 4 2

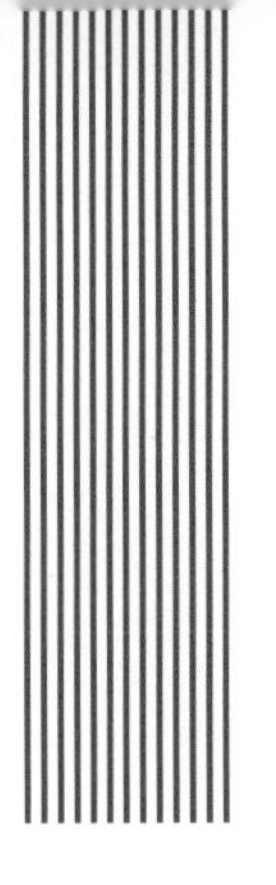

Contents

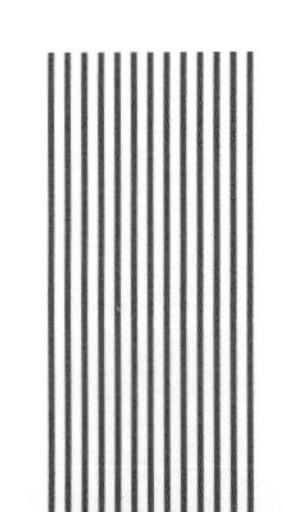

A NOTE FROM THE EDITORS

Caution: This book has been proven to cause laugh lines.

But what's a little wrinkle or a few extra crow's feet compared with the sheer joy that will spread across your face with each flip of the page? As you journey through the chapters ahead, you can look forward to a prescription-strength mood boost, a bright smile and twinkling eyes, plus a ready supply of back-pocket one-liners, quotable quotes and kitchen-table gags that will stick with you for years to come.

With a history spanning more than a century, after all, *Reader's Digest* knows timeless humor. In the magazine's beloved humor columns—namely Laughter the Best Medicine, All in a Day's Work, Humor in Uniform and Life in These United States—readers, tweeters, comedians and other jokesters all shine a spotlight on the myriad moments that make each day worth smiling about: hearing an unwittingly hilarious comment from a little tyke in your life, making a workplace flub so embarrassing you just have to laugh, coming home to the zany high jinks of a furry friend and so much more.

This book features the cream of the crop from that *Reader's Digest* joke archive, with bonus material from some of our sister publications, classic cartoons sure to make you smile, and essays from seasoned humorists that tease out new (and funny) perspectives on our shared experiences.

In "Telepathy with ... My Dog?", for example, writer Patricia Pearson finds herself at an impasse with her family dog, Kevin, whose inscrutable communication techniques (read: blank stares) leave his owners mystified. Looking to unlock the secret to animal-speak—and getting nowhere with treats and walks—Pearson enlists the help of a quirky pet telepathist, with mixed results.

Sometimes the key to effective communication is just faking it until you make it. Ask Canadian writer Sophie Kohn, who in her essay "Hockey Talk" learns to blend in with her hockey-holic colleagues by using stock phrases supplied by a sympathetic friend. Or take a cue from the regular Joes with celebrity names featured in Lenore Skenazy's piece "Funny, You Don't Look like Daniel Craig." Kelly Clarkson and Michael Jordan—but not *that* Kelly Clarkson or *that* Michael Jordan—still reap some big benefits when booking hotels and making dinner reservations, but reality comes crashing down the minute their true identities are revealed.

If real celebrity is what you're after, however, there's no cause for concern. In each chapter of this book you will spot quotable quotes from comedy giants such as Steve Martin, Gilda Radner, Conan O'Brien and Erma Bombeck, as well as other celebrities known for their sizzling wit. No matter the contributor, all the gags ahead are worth their weight in comedy gold—and if you ask us, we think they're worth the laugh lines too.

—THE EDITORS OF *READER'S DIGEST*

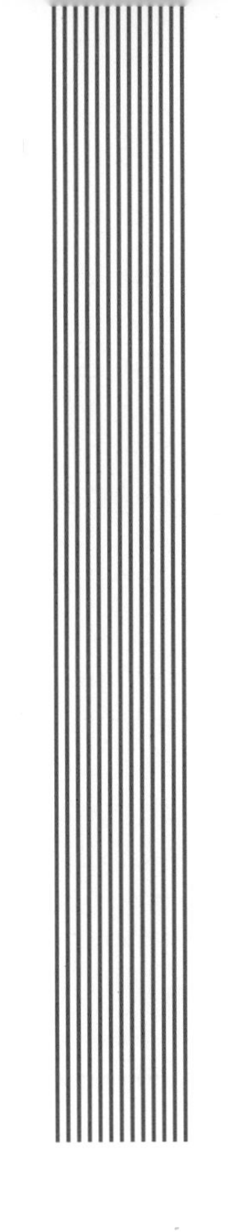

IN THE
MONEY

When my local barista handed me my change, one coin stood out.

"Look at that. You rarely get one of these old wheat pennies nowadays," I said, tapping the sheaf-of-wheat design. I handed her the penny.

Turning it over and over in her hand, she said, "You know, I always thought they were made of copper."

—LINDA NEUKRUG

St. Thomas, in the Virgin Islands, is famous for stunning and affordable jewelry. A day before our cruise ship approached the port, a fellow passenger asked the cruise director what time the jewelry stores open. We had plenty of time, he assured her: "They open as soon as they hear our anchor go *splash*."

—MARK ROBERTS

Gus took four tires to a friend's garage sale and was asking $35 apiece. He needed to step away for a bit, so he asked his friend to watch the tires for him.

"In case someone offers less, how low are you willing to go?" the friend asked.

"Try for more, but I'll accept $20 each," Gus said, and left. When he returned, the tires were gone.

"How much did you get for them?" Gus asked excitedly.

"Twenty bucks each."

"Oh, OK. And who bought them?"

"I did!"

—R.S.

A last-minute filer walked into our state income tax office and handed me his returns. Just as he did, a peal of laughter could be heard in another room. Glaring at me, he grumbled, "What are they doing back there, counting the money?"

—WILLIAM UMBERSON

The only time I am truly present is when my credit card is in the card reader and I'm waiting for it to be approved.

—@BILLDIXONISH

I took my 8-year-old nephew, Kerry, to an Easter church service. When the collection plate came by, Kerry added his offering and I added mine. Then Kerry leaned close and commented, "You'd think God would have enough money by now."

—JOHN LOUMP

"You call THAT the trappings of wealth?"

I would like to think that money won't change me, but I won $5 on a scratch-off lottery ticket and immediately bought brand-name aluminum foil.

—@ABBYHASISSUES

Freelance newspaper writers don't get nearly as much attention as writers with regular bylines. So I was delighted when I finally got some notice. It was at the bank, and I was depositing a stack of checks.

"Wow," said the teller, reading off the names of publishers from the tops of the checks. "You must deliver a lot of papers."

—MEAGAN FRANCIS

I tried having my mother's phone disconnected, but the customer service representative told me that since the account was in my dad's name, he'd have to be the one to put in the request. The fact that he had been dead for 40 years didn't sway her. Then a solution hit me: "If I stop paying the bill, you can turn off the service, right?"

"Well, yes," she said reluctantly. "But that would ruin his credit."

—JEANNIE GIBBS

In 1984, my sister's husband worked for GTE servicing small relay stations around Redmond, Washington. He suggested we buy stock in a company that was one of his clients. So I bought 200 shares, as did my mom. We watched the stock go up to around $31 a share and then drop again. Then it would go back up and drop again. My old accounting professor had told the class that if we had a stock that performed that way, it probably would never go higher and we should dump it. So that's why Mom and I sold our stock in Microsoft at under $31 a share. I never look at what it is today, because I don't want to be sick.

—K.W.

Quick Quips

I'm well prepared for a cashless society. Having kids already has me there.

—@KENTWGRAHAM

If you want to know what it's like to owe a loan shark, borrow $5 from a 10-year-old.

—@SLADEWENTWORTH

The only exercise I've done this month is running out of money.

—@COLLEGESTUDENT

Please don't come to my garage sale if you've ever let me borrow something.

—@MJKSPEAKS

I have an idea for a hot wings restaurant: The wings are free, but napkins cost $100.

—@LUNCH_ENJOYER

First of the month coming up soon? Don't use one of these excuses tenants gave their landlords for not paying the rent:

- "I have to make payments on my BMW and iPhones."
- "You are too wrapped up in the whole concept of 'money.'"
- "So ... you're talking to me only because the rent's not paid? Is that all I am to you? A tenant?"

—THE LANDLORD PROTECTION AGENCY

I say "I have money tied up in investments" to describe returns I haven't sent back yet.

—@LUCYJ_FORD

The rainbow was on your property, Mr. O'Toole, so technically, you are responsible for claiming the gold as personal income.
INTERNAL REVENUE
AUDIT
Luck of the IRS
Reynolds

At the Christmas Eve service at my church, the pastor, quizzing some children about the Nativity, asked, "What gifts did the three wise men give the Christ child?"

"Gold!" one child yelled excitedly.

"Frankincense!" shouted another.

After a pause, a third asked, "Gift cards?"

—ALAN SHAW

Who says that corporate executives are boring? These companies clearly had some fun selecting their stock exchange symbols:

- **BID:** Sotheby's, the auction company
- **CAKE:** The Cheesecake Factory
- **FIZZ:** National Beverage Company
- **HOG:** Harley-Davidson Motorcycles
- **PZZA:** Papa John's
- **ZEUS:** Olympic Steel Inc.

A woman approached me at the bank wanting to buy a savings bond for her granddaughter, who was soon to be baptized. Not sure how much she wanted to spend, I asked, "What denomination?"

She responded, "Protestant."

—BARBARA CONAGE

The barber's client looked depressed, so the barber told him, "Cheer up. I knew a guy who owed $5,000 he couldn't pay. He drove his vehicle to the edge of a cliff, where he sat for over an hour. A group of concerned citizens heard about his problem and passed a hat around. Relieved, the man pulled back from the cliff's edge."

"Incredible," said the client. "Who were these kind people?"

"The passengers on the bus."

—PATRICK BROOME

"Don't do that," I said when one of my first graders playfully draped a dollar bill over his eyes. "Money is full of germs."

"It is?" he asked.

"Yes, it's very dirty."

He thought about it for a moment, then said, "Is that why they call people who have a lot of it filthy rich?"

—ELIZABETH WEBBER

If HGTV has taught me anything, it's that the key to happiness is an open-concept layout, double sinks in the bathroom, a kitchen island the size of Hawaii and a $1.2 million budget.

—@ABBYHASISSUES

YARD SALES: WHAT A WAY TO MAKE A BUCK!

When you peddle your possessions off to the neighbors, you might find that your priceless stuff isn't so priceless after all

By Will Stanton

A **man never** realizes how ruthless a wife can be until she holds a yard sale. Nothing is sacred. A *Hardy Boys* set in mint condition, a Turkish water pipe, a rowing machine. A *rowing machine*?

"Maggie!" I cried.

"You never use it," she said.

"So what?" I said. "If it comes to that, I don't *use* my stuffed marsh hawk or my Walt Dropo autographed baseball." She said not to go so fast. Too late, I realized she was jotting down a list.

For years, Maggie had threatened to hold a yard sale. I'd thought that was all it was—a threat. But now she was clearing out the sun porch and collecting stuff from around the house.

"If there's something you really want to keep, just tell me," she said. "No need to sneak it out like whatever it is you're hiding under your newspaper."

I told her I wasn't hiding anything. "I just picked up this cigar case to take a better look."

"If you want to keep it—"

"You've priced it at a dime. It's worth at least 30 cents."

She said the whole point of a yard sale was to get rid of stuff.

Yes, I said, but not to give it away.

"I'll make it 15 cents," she said.

She asked me to price the books, so I had to go through half a dozen cartons of them with a 10-year accumulation of attic dust. Before I finished, the phone rang. Maggie wanted to know who it was.

"Mac wanted me to come over for a beer," I said. "I told him I was busy sorting cartons of dirty books."

"Oh yes?" Maggie said.

"He said he'd be right over."

When Maggie told our boys about the sale, they greeted it with the same enthusiasm they would have shown for harp lessons or a dentist appointment. Their contributions were three jigsaw puzzles in one box, a bag of old flashlight batteries and one imitation-leather gun belt that had wintered under a forsythia bush.

I told them I didn't see how they were going to make much money that way. Roy looked at Sammy. Sammy looked at Roy. Both looked at me. They could keep the money?

"It's your stuff," I said.

It was touching. A moment that comes but once to every American parent—when he sees the first gleam of capitalism in his child's eye.

Luckily, Maggie caught them before they could strip their room.

The week before the sale, the weather was unsettled. We checked the reports hourly. I could appreciate how Eisenhower had felt as D-Day approached. Our rummage was massed along a broad front, a heavy buildup of old clothes in the parlor, a concentration of bric-a-brac on the sun porch. Kitchenware was assigned to the hallway and set to move out in the first wave if the weather held.

The sale was scheduled for Saturday morning, but as soon as we put the word out on Friday, people started calling. Did we have antique furniture, pictures, china? Maggie said no, only ordinary, middle-class debris.

> **"What did they expect for 15 cents—Xanadu?"**

They came before the sale started, poking around, turning things over to see where they had been made. A young woman with no makeup showed her husband the bottom of a shipping case. "Trenton," she said, and both snickered. What did they expect for 15 cents—Xanadu?

An expensively dressed couple tumbled the merchandise—strewing books, dislodging knickknacks—to remarks of a disparaging nature. Finally the woman offered to pay half price for several small items. Maggie said she wasn't ready yet to cut prices. The woman said with a sweet smile that she might have to with goods of such poor quality—nothing for a serious collector.

Maggie returned the smile and said it was too bad they hadn't come an hour earlier, before we'd sold all the Delft china. Delft? the woman said. Yes, Maggie said, old dishes.

Some fellow had bought a boxful. The woman grasped the door for support. How could Maggie have sold the best things before the sale even started?

Maggie patted her shoulder and said, "If you want to be a serious collector, you're going to have to force yourself to be pushier."

A yard sale is a traumatic experience. Even your best stuff looks tacky in bright sunlight, and these things are far from your best. These are the mistakes and bad guesses of a lifetime. All weekend, you're surrounded by memories you'd rather forget.

I called to a friend of Maggie's. She gave me a decidedly frosty look and stalked by. I asked Maggie, "What's wrong with Esme?" It turned out that Esme had been browsing at the trinket counter and had found a statuette of a man in a floppy hat riding a burro. Maggie realized—too late—that it was a bridge prize she had won. At Esme's.

"What could I say?" Maggie asked. "I told her I'd been hunting for it high and low and that *you* must have put it there. She probably won't speak to you for a year."

Of course, there were a lot of presents we had given each other. Just because we had them for sale didn't mean we were unfeeling about them. After all, it's the thought that counts, and it annoyed me to watch people rummaging heedlessly through things we had selected with so much care.

You can learn a lot about people from a yard sale. Maggie says the main thing you learn is that you never know. Spendthrifts on Fifth Avenue are cheapskates in your backyard. One woman with a diamond as big as a bumblebee spent 15 minutes beating me down on a 25-cent tin tray.

Then an old fellow asked the price of an electric blanket. He had on a sweater with the elbows missing, and his eyeglasses were mended with tape. When I quoted him $2.75, he opened his change purse and started counting out nickels and dimes. I was so fed up with rich hagglers that this got to me.

"I must have misread that tag," I said. "It's 75 cents, not $2.75." You'd have thought I had given him a gold watch. He was so grateful, it was touching.

I told Maggie about it. "He was such a nice change from the chiselers." I told her about the woman with the diamond.

"A redheaded woman?" Maggie asked. "In canary-colored slacks? That wasn't a real diamond. I just sold it to her for 20 cents."

I was making a mental apology to the diamond lady when I saw the old fellow with the blanket driving away—in a Mercedes. As Maggie says, you never know.

"Isn't it enough we tip well? Must we also like him on Facebook and follow him on Twitter?"

One of the shortest wills ever written: "Being of sound mind, I spent all the money."

—ARTHUR BLAND

I've started restoring furniture and then selling it on Facebook in order to finance my expensive new hobby, which is restoring furniture to sell on Facebook.

—@LMEGORDON

My uncle is a frugal man. He once told the woman at the movie theater box office that since he couldn't remember if he'd seen the film, he wouldn't buy a ticket until he was sure. And with that, he marched inside and found a seat.

A half-hour later, the manager, followed by two police officers, collared him. As they escorted him out, my uncle shouted, "I'm still not sure whether I saw this!"

—MARY ANN VERGETIS

One day at the bank where I worked as a teller, an elderly gentleman presented me with a check; unfortunately, he had no ID. Keenly aware of the growing line behind him, he dug through his pockets to no avail. Suddenly his face lit up. He grinned and pointed to his head.

"There's my name on my cap!"

Sure enough, the name on his hat was the same as the one on the check. Then he leaned forward and whispered conspiratorially, "Actually, it's my son's cap, but we've got the same name."

—GRACE DIFALCO

While spending the day at Mount Rushmore, I decided to get lunch from a stand being worked by Boy Scouts. The three hot dogs I ordered cost $4 each, and I also picked up beverages worth $7.

"That'll be $10," said the young Scout ringing up my order.

Recognizing his math error, I said, "You might want to try that again, son."

A look of realization dawned across his face. He smiled wide and replied, "That'll be $10, *please*."

—JIM MOELLER

A woman at our checkout counter didn't have enough money to cover her purchase of toilet paper, so I paid the remaining 96 cents.

"Thank you so much," she said. "I'm going to think of you every time I use this paper."

—RICHARD F. PFEIFER

Tip-jar humor in our local coffee shop: "Afraid of Change? Leave It Here."

—PAULA HASSLER

I laughingly threatened my 8-year-old with coal for Christmas and, without missing a beat, he replied, "You mean my future diamonds?"

—@CRANKYPANTSKNIT

Me: Can I borrow 50 bucks?

Mom: You don't call to say hi, and you didn't call on my birthday. All you ever call for is money!

Me: Forty bucks?

Mom: OK.

—CRAZYTHINGSPARENTSTEXT.COM

Before cellphones, I was in Manhattan to visit my brother. Stopping at a pay phone to call him, I reached into my wallet for a scrap of paper with his number on it.

When I got to his place, he greeted me with "So, you lost your wallet." A woman had just called him, saying she had found the wallet with his phone number inside. She was sitting in a bar and gave him the address. I hurried over and found my hero.

"May I buy you a drink?" I asked.

"Oh, that's sweet, dear," she said, handing me my wallet. "But you don't have enough money."

—MICHAEL HAUPTMAN IN *THE NEW YORK TIMES*

Gambling Addiction

A woman won $25,000 after entering a sweepstakes at an Illinois gambling parlor. Good for her, except that she happens to be a prominent anti-gambling crusader, having gone after casinos, a VFW raffle and even the parent company of the gambling parlor where she won. Still, she insists she's not a hypocrite: Her winnings are a result of her crusade. "It's God showing his grace on me."

—*CHICAGO TRIBUNE*

Working as an apartment manager, I've heard every excuse for why the rent is late: Husband got laid off. Kids were sick. I lost the money order. Or simply, "I forgot." But the most creative excuse of all was this: "I had only half the rent. So I went up to the casino to try to double my money."

—MIKKI SAMS

An elderly friend of mine, a staunch Baptist, told me that when she visited Las Vegas with her family, she was persuaded to try the slot machines. I asked if she said a quick prayer before playing.

"Oh no," she said. "I figured when I walked through that door, I was on my own."

—CAPERS CROSS

Lying on his deathbed, the rich, miserly old man calls to his long-suffering wife.

"I want to take all my money with me," he tells her. "So promise me you'll put it in the casket."

After the man dies, his widow attends the memorial service with her best friend. Just before the undertaker closes the coffin, she places a small metal box inside.

Her friend looks at her in horror. "Surely," she says, "you didn't put the money in there."

"I did promise him I would," the widow answers. "So I got it all together, deposited every penny in my account and wrote him a check. If he can cash it, he can spend it."

—UNKNOWN

I was in a job interview today. The interviewer handed me his laptop and said, "I want you to try to sell this to me." So I put it under my arm, walked out of the building and went home. Eventually he called and demanded, "Bring it back here right now!" I said, "Three hundred bucks and it's yours."

—BLOG.ZOOMINFO.COM

A plumber fixes a leak in a doctor's house, then bills him for $1,000. "This is ridiculous!" the doctor says. "I don't even charge that much." The plumber says, "Neither did I when I was a doctor."

—THEPLUMBINGINFO.COM

The quickest way to double your money is to fold it and put it in your back pocket.

—WILL ROGERS

When tax time comes around, don't try these excuses for being late; they didn't work the first time they were used.

- "I could not complete my tax return because my husband left me and took our accountant with him."
- "I haven't had time because a baby magpie flew into my house and I have to stay in to feed it."
- "I suffer from late-filing syndrome."
- "A wasp in my car caused me to have an accident, and my tax return, which was inside, was destroyed."

—*THE TELEGRAPH* AND ACCOUNTINGWEB.CO.UK

When my youngest nephew was 7, he came home confused about whether or not to believe in Santa because some kids at school told him there was no such thing. When my brother asked my nephew what he thought, his response was, "There has to be a Santa, because you could never afford all this stuff."

—CAROL FEELEY

The average U.S. household is worth $118,200. Amazon founder Jeff Bezos is worth about $172 billion. That's like comparing:

- The size of a white blood cell to the size of a finback whale.
- The height of a piece of Toblerone chocolate to the height of five Mount Everests.
- The length of a single adult stride to the distance from New York to Kentucky.
- The volume of a quiet library to the roar of a (private) jet taking off.

—*THE NEW YORK TIMES*

The manager of a jewelry store nabs a shoplifter trying to steal a necklace.

"Listen," the crook says, "you don't want any trouble, and neither do I. What if I just buy the necklace and we forget this happened?"

The manager agrees and writes a sales slip.

"You know," says the crook, looking at the price, "this is more than I wanted to spend. Got anything less expensive?"

—ROSEMARY COVERT

My wife does this cute thing now and then where she goes out shopping for next year's yard sale items.

—@CRAVIN4

A frugal widow goes to the newspaper office to take out an obituary notice for her late husband.

"How much?" she asks the fellow behind the counter.

"It's one dollar per word," he says.

She says, "Make it 'MacGregor died.'"

"It's a five-word minimum."

She nearly faints but collects herself.

"Very well. Make it 'MacGregor died. Volvo for sale.'"

—CHRISTOPHER BUCKLEY

A banker approaches the Pearly Gates sweating and struggling with a heavy suitcase. St. Peter greets him and says, "Set the suitcase down and come in."

"No way!" barks the banker. "I have to bring it in."

"What could possibly be in there that's so important?" St. Peter asks.

The banker opens the suitcase to reveal 50 gold bricks. St. Peter's jaw drops: "You brought pavement?"

—JIMMY HOLMES

Elon Musk is now worth $208 billion.
You want to know how he did it?
He skipped 34.67 billion lattes. It's that easy.

—@STEPHENPUNWASI

"Dear, did something happen at the office?"

After two days of heated wrangling, we got one of our vendors to agree to a 35% discount. As we were about to sign the contract, my boss, who had not been a party to the negotiations, walked in and tore it up, saying, "I'm going to teach you purchasing people how to play hardball. That's the way you make it in this world." He turned to the vendor's sales rep and said, "We want a 20% discount; take it or leave it." The delighted rep immediately agreed. As my boss left, he said to us, "I hope you learned something from that."

—INC.COM

I went to Bank of America to deposit a check, and they asked me for ID. I said, "Are you telling me other people are trying to put money into my account and you're telling them no?"

—RICH VOS IN *THE WALL STREET JOURNAL*

During a job interview at the 99 Cents store, my son was asked, "Where do you see yourself in five years?" My son's reply: "At the Dollar Store." He got the job.

—A.K.

"I'll need the saw again, sir."

As the hedge fund manager steps out of his Porsche, a truck goes racing by, taking the door off the hinges.

"My Porsche! My beautiful silver Porsche is ruined!" he screams.

A police officer on the scene shakes his head in disgust.

"Unbelievable," he says. "You're so focused on your possessions that you didn't even realize your left arm was shorn off when the truck hit you."

The distraught man looks down in absolute horror.

"Oh, no!" he cries. "My Rolex!"

—WATCHUSEEK.COM

A wealthy businessman liked to show his party guests his pool and say, "If you swim a lap, I will give you $10 million, half of my estate or my daughter's hand in marriage. But there's a shark in the pool."

One day as he said this, there was a loud splash. A man swam a lap of the pool and got out just as the shark thudded into the wall.

"So, would you like the $10 million?"

"No," the man said.

"Half of my estate?"

"No," the man said.

"Ah! You want to marry my daughter."

"No! I want the name of the man who pushed me in!"

—ALPHAUSA.ORG

The biggest change after having kids was putting a swear jar in the house. Whenever I say a bad word, I have to put a dollar in the jar, and at the end of every month, I take all that money and buy myself a nice steak for being such a cool dad.

—MARK CHALIFOUX

Tyler, my 4-year-old son, went to a local baseball game with my mother-in-law. At the park, she gave him money to buy a treat from the concession booth. When he returned, she asked him for the change.

Tyler patted his pocket. "This is mine," he stated. Pointing to the woman in the booth, he added, "She has yours."

—KELLY CHRISTO

Our utility customers often don't understand the intricacies of their bills. Recently, a man called asking how much he owed.

"Actually," I said, "you have a credit for $98.70."

"So that means that I am ahead on my bill?" he asked.

"That's right!"

After a pause: "And when is that due?"

—TIFFANY JEW

Never keep up with the Joneses. Drag them down to your level. It's cheaper.

—QUENTIN CRISP

QUOTABLE QUOTES

WHOEVER SAID MONEY CAN'T BUY HAPPINESS SIMPLY DIDN'T KNOW WHERE TO GO SHOPPING.

—BO DEREK

Why is there so much month left at the end of the money?

—JOHN BARRYMORE

I'm spending a year dead for tax reasons.

—DOUGLAS ADAMS

A bank is a place that will lend you money if you can prove that you don't need it.

—BOB HOPE

I don't care how much money you have, free stuff is always a good thing.

—QUEEN LATIFAH

A study of economics usually reveals that the best time to buy anything is last year.

—MARTY ALLEN

People will buy anything that is one to a customer.

—SINCLAIR LEWIS

Why pay a dollar for a bookmark? Why not use the dollar for a bookmark?

—STEVEN SPIELBERG

Dogs have no money. Isn't that amazing? They're broke their entire lives. But they get through. You know why dogs have no money? No pockets.

—JERRY SEINFELD

It's better to do nothing with your money than something you don't understand.

—SUZE ORMAN

I THINK IT'S WRONG THAT ONLY ONE COMPANY MAKES THE GAME MONOPOLY.

—STEVEN WRIGHT

THEIR PRODUCT HAD A SHORT SHELF LIFE

An interested buyer could smell a bargain

By Adam Sibcy

own the street from my old house in Darlington, South Carolina, was a pond where, one day in the summer of 1976, my friend Danny and I decided to try rig fishing. I'd read about the technique in *Field & Stream*: You attach a baited line to an overhanging tree branch, and when the fish hits the line, it sets the hook. We baited the rig line with a smaller fish and bided our time upstream.

Meanwhile Danny's brother David showed up with a few friends. They weren't all that interested in our fishing experiment—that is, until it worked. With a loud *bam!* the tree limb slapped the water with the weight of a huge fish.

We got it onto the bank and saw that it was a mudfish—as long as my leg!

One of the boys suggested we sell it in town. Some of the old locals love this type of fish, he said, and they know how to clean it. So Danny and I picked up our catch, and the five of us headed into town about a mile away.

We hit a live one at our first stop.

"That's a good fish you got there," the shop owner said. "I'll give you $3 for it, split five ways."

"But Danny and I were the ones who caught it," I protested. "These other guys were just spectators."

The man was firm. "Share the money or no deal."

Danny and I thought about it and decided it was no deal. We lugged that smelly thing around town, store to store, the rest of the afternoon—and guess what? No one else was interested in a dead mudfish.

So we ended up back at the first shop. The owner was still willing to take it—but at a new price. This time, he offered us the grand sum of $1.

Danny and I didn't even have to think about it. Deal!

2

THE ANIMAL KINGDOM

One beautiful morning, my husband and I decided to go for a drive in the country. Unfortunately, no matter which road we took, we kept seeing dead possums lying on the shoulder. After several miles of this, my husband turned to me and said, "Now I think I know the answer to the age-old question 'Why did the chicken cross the road?'"

"What is it?" I asked.

"Well," he replied, "it was to prove to the possums that it could be done."

—JUANITA PAGE

I love overhearing pet owners talking to their dogs. Recently, I was petting a pup who seemed happy until he suddenly growled at me. Alarmed, I got up and left. As I turned a corner, I heard his owner quietly reproach him: "You always do this, Oscar. You drive away all your friends."

—@JULIAGALEF

"Can I purchase frogs for my new pond here?" a customer asked at our garden center.

"You don't need to buy frogs," I explained. "They just sort of choose where to live, and then they turn up."

"Right ..." agreed the gentleman. "And is the same true with fish?"

—SAMANTHA DAVIS

A turtle walks into a bar and orders a glass of water. The bartender hands the turtle the water and watches it slowly walk off. The next day, the turtle returns, orders another glass of water and, again, inches away. This goes on for a few days until the bartender finally asks, "Instead of water, wouldn't you like a beer? A snack?"

"Not now!" shouts the turtle. "My house is on fire!"

—REDDIT.COM

I walked into our living room and found our expensive decorative sofa pillow in shreds. I asked my teenage daughter whether she knew which of our three dogs was responsible.

"It was Cotton," she said nonchalantly.

"How do you know?"

"I watched him."

—TONY BUNKER

Our cat, Ceremony, is mostly referred to as Cat. When we have a visitor, though, we revert to her real name so that we can say, "Come in, but don't stand on Ceremony."

—@7UPISLEMONADE

Give your canine a leg up in our dog-eat-dog world by naming him or her after someone famous. Here's some inspiration collected by care.com:

- Kareem Abdul-Jabbark
- Droolius Caesar
- Woofgang Amadeus Mozart
- Sarah Jessica Barker
- Jimmy Chew

A friend's 5-year-old saw a rhino and called it a battle unicorn. Can we let 5-year-olds christen new species, please?

—@ZOESZOOYOUTUBE

Living in a household with eight indoor cats requires buying large amounts of kitty litter, which I usually get in 25-pound bags—100 pounds at a time. When I was going to be out of town for a week, I decided to go to the supermarket to stock up. As my husband and I pushed shopping carts, each cart loaded with five large bags of litter, a man looked at our purchases and queried, "Bengal or Siberian?"

—JUDY J. HAGG

I spend three minutes every day choosing a TV channel to leave on for my dog, then I go to work and people take me seriously as an adult.

—@DAMIENFAHEY

Horse Sense

"We've traced the call. It's coming from INSIDE THE HORSE!" —Trojan 911 dispatcher

—@EWFEEZ

You can lead a horse to water, but you need a seahorse to continue your journey.

—@SHARKJELLY

If I ever got a horse, I would name her Grace, just in case I ever fell from her.

—@3SUNZZZ

I bet on a great horse yesterday! It took seven horses to beat him.

—@BRYCEEGIBBS

Do other animals have signature tranquilizers, or are horses just especially stressed out?

—@ATANENHAUS

"Um."—First horse that got ridden

—@RORYNOTROY

"I wish they would stop putting food in my hat."

Employees at a Spanish zoo conducted an emergency drill that simulated a gorilla escape. To make it more realistic, a zookeeper dressed up as an ape and took off. Unfortunately, not everyone on staff was notified about the drill. Upon seeing a fleeing "gorilla," one of the zoo veterinarians grabbed a tranquilizer gun and shot the employee in the leg.

—THEDODO.COM

I work at a pet supply store. A customer once called to set up a delivery. Among the items he wanted was a dog toy, but he didn't know which one. I had to pick out toys and squeak them into the phone for him until he heard the "right one."

—@KRISTINNEUMAN

At a workshop on dog temperament, the instructor noted that a test for a canine's disposition was for the owner to fall down and act hurt. A dog with poor temperament would try to bite the person, whereas a good dog would lick its owner's face or show concern. Once, while eating pizza in the living room, I decided to try out this theory on my two dogs. I stood up, clutched my heart, let out a scream and collapsed on the floor. The dogs looked at me, glanced at each other and raced to the coffee table for my pizza.

—SUSAN MOTTICE

Actual calls that cops have responded to that had nothing to do with humans, save for the dodos who phoned them in:

- A man reported that his neighbor's dog is a jerk.
- A resident worried that a noisy hawk in a tree was in some sort of distress. When authorities arrived, the hawk was quiet and enjoying dinner.
- A caller reported that a belligerent squirrel was preventing him from using his boat dock. The caller said he knew nothing could be done about it, but he wanted officers to know "what kind of squirrels are running about in the community."
- Police responded to a report of two dogs running loose and attacking ducks. One duck refused medical treatment and left the area.
- Dispatch reported "a Swanson chicken potpie running east on Clay Street."

—POLICEONE.COM, FLATHEADBEACON.COM AND GAWKER.COM

I just spent 15 minutes liking photos of dogs on Instagram. Time well spent.

—@JEREMYADAMROSS

STRANGER THINGS

Every species has its peculiarities, but some creatures are just weirder than others

By Andy Simmons

In the name of self-preservation, mating and even lunch, many animals have developed some curious—make that horrifying—habits. A female praying mantis biting the head off her lover is among the most extreme examples, but there are plenty of creatures that have pushed the envelope of good taste in less murderous ways. Check out a menagerie that's so gross, other beasts might shake their heads and declare, "That's disgusting!"

EURASIAN ROLLER BIRD

Imagine you saw some people to whom you wanted to say hello, but as you approached, they opened their mouths—and vomited on you. You would give them a wide berth, right? Young Eurasian roller birds have a good reason for this rude behavior: They assumed you were going to eat them. Rollers have been known to travel from Europe to central Asia, and along the way they encounter countless snakes and other predators. When the young birds hurl their orange, putrid-smelling intestinal fluid, it deters the bad guys and alerts their parents to potential trouble.

HAIRY FROG

If you learned of a frog that was constantly breaking its bones, you might think, *Wow, that's one careless critter*. But the 4-inch hairy frog of central Africa knows what it's doing. When threatened, it can contract muscles that are connected to its hind claws, breaking the toe bones. The frog then thrusts the shards through its toe pads, turning them into weapons. When the foe has been vanquished, the bones retreat back into the foot, where it's believed the tissue around the bony claws eventually regenerates. Superhero fans may recognize this move. After all, the creature's nom de guerre is the wolverine frog.

SEA CUCUMBER

The sea cucumber's slothlike speed should make it easy prey. But this bottom feeder possesses a secret weapon. When under threat by, say, a crab, some sea cucumber species shoot out their guts—their intestines, respiratory tracts and even their reproductive organs!—from their anuses. Believe it or not, certain predators find this appetizing. As the predator digs in, the sea cucumber hides under a rock or in the sand and plots its escape. Afterward the sea cucumber finds itself in a kind of suspended animation for a few months, regenerating its organs. Talk about spilling your guts!

BOMBARDIER BEETLE

Forget John, Paul, George and Ringo—this is true beetlemania. The bombardier beetle fends off attackers by bombing them with chemicals hot enough to burn human skin. The flying half-inch creature has two separate glands. One contains hydroquinone, which also can be engineered in a lab and is used commercially as a skin-bleaching agent, and hydrogen peroxide. The other harbors a mixture of enzymes. When the glands' contents are mixed, they create a chemical that can reach a temperature of 212 degrees. The beetle then shoots this combination out from a nozzle-like opening on the rear of its abdomen up to 20 times in a row.

HONEY BADGER

The 30-pound honey badger has been dubbed the most fearless animal in the world for its willingness to take on larger beasts, such as lions and buffaloes. Aside from an incredibly powerful jaw and a thick, rubbery skin, the honey badger defends itself by turning the pouch in its rear end inside out to spray enemies with a suffocating stench. This action sends predators fleeing, which is exactly what you would do if someone you just met pulled the same stunt. Here's another factoid: The honey badger usually lives alone. Gee, wonder why.

XENOMORPH WASP

Remember the film *Alien*? The title character, a creature called a xenomorph, injects its embryo into the body of an astronaut. A few days later ... *Bam!* A baby alien pops out of the poor guy's chest. Well, a researcher in Australia discovered a wasp that injects its eggs into its victim, such as a moth caterpillar. After hatching, the wasp's young consume the caterpillar's insides, then burst out of its body as fully formed larvae. Sometimes the caterpillar survives in a zombified state, doomed to live out its life protecting the new communal cocoon until the day the larvae emerge as adult wasps. The researcher, obviously a sci-fi fan, dubbed the wasp *Dolichogenidea xenomorph*. Think of it as another sequel in the *Alien* canon.

"Waterproof, great for winter, comes in brown only." When Shervin Hess of the Oregon Zoo read this product review for hiking boots, he realized it also described sea otters. The Association of Zoos and Aquariums picked up on his idea and published an entire collection called *Animals Reviewed.* Here are a few of their ratings:

- **Linnaeus's two-toed sloth:** 2 stars. Built-in hooks make it easy to hang, but it quickly runs out of power and needs most of a day to recharge.
- **Blue-and-gold macaw:** 3 stars. Cool colors, but the playback feature sometimes doesn't work, and there is no volume control. Plus, it might peck at you if you try to fast-forward.
- **Giant anteater:** 4 stars. Works well in hard-to-reach places. The nozzle does NOT detach. Leaves a slimy residue, but it comes with a bonus duster on the back.
- **Giant Pacific octopus:** 5 stars. Customizable color blends easily with any decor. Suction cups secure to any surface, even underwater.

One of my young son's friends called us on FaceTime. "I got some really bad news," the friend said in a solemn tone. Concerned, I listened closely. My son asked, "What happened?"

His friend said, "Jeff died today."

My wife, also concerned, asked, "Who's Jeff?"

"He's my frog," the friend replied. He then said a sweet prayer about the frog, saying he was thankful for their time on earth together and for the joy Jeff brought to their lives. It was a pretty mature eulogy for a kid. He ended it with "Amen." Before I could raise my bowed head, the toilet flushed.

—JUSTIN JUKNELIS

Had a job walking five chihuahuas. When they got tired, I had to carry them home: two in my arms, two on my shoulders and one on my head.

—@WHOOPIEPIE10

On a Facebook page for beginning artists, one asked, "Any suggestions for painting dogs?" Another responded, "Wait till they're asleep."

—LYNETTE COMBS

"Lick. Lick. Lick. Lick. Lick. Lick. Lick. Lick. Lick. Lick. Lick. Lick. Lick. Lick. Lick. Lick. Lick. Lick. Then I thought, why not take a real bath?"

Science tip: You can distinguish an alligator from a crocodile by paying attention to whether the animal sees you later or in a while.

—@GOOOOATS

A kangaroo kept getting out of its enclosure at the zoo. Knowing it could hop high, the zookeepers put up a 10-foot fence. Didn't matter—the kangaroo was out the next morning, hopping about. So a 20-foot fence was put up. Again, it got out. When the fence was 40 feet high, a camel in the next enclosure asked the kangaroo, "How high do you think they'll go?"

The kangaroo said, "A thousand feet—unless somebody locks the gate at night."

—GCFL.NET

In his younger days, our family's golden retriever, Catcher, often ran away when he had the chance. His veterinarian's office was about a mile down the road, and Catcher would usually end up there. The office staff knew him well and would call me to come pick him up. One day I called the vet to make an appointment for Catcher's yearly vaccine.

"Will you be bringing him?" the receptionist asked. "Or will he be coming on his own?"

—LAURA STASZAK

Apartment life often means little privacy. I realized that fact one day when my kitten was running around my bedroom, climbing onto shelves and into the dresser as I was getting ready for work. I finally yelled at the kitten: "You'd better sit down! You're getting on my nerves!" A second later, a voice from upstairs responded, "OK!"

—LADONNA DANIELSON HUGHETT

One of the highlights of the freshman biology class at New Mexico Highlands University was the monthly feeding of a caged rattlesnake kept in the laboratory. One time, the entire class gathered around the cage and, in complete silence, watched as the feeding took place.

"I'm jealous of the snake," the instructor said. "I never get the class's undivided attention like this."

A student answered, matter-of-factly, "You would if you could swallow a mouse."

—DIANE TALBOTT-MOSIER

If you can sit quietly after difficult news, if in financial downturns you remain perfectly calm, if you can see your neighbors travel to fantastic places without a twinge of jealousy, if you can eat happily whatever is put on your plate, if you can fall asleep after a day of running around without a drink or a pill, if you can always find contentment just where you are—you are probably a dog.

—JACK KORNFIELD

The vet prescribed daily tablets for our geriatric cat, Tigger, and after several battles my husband devised a way to give her the medication. It involved wrapping Tigger in a towel, trapping her between his knees, forcing her mouth open and depositing the pill on the back of her tongue. David was proud of his resourcefulness until one hectic session when he lost control of both the cat and the medicine. Tigger leaped out of his grasp, paused to inspect the tablet—which had rolled across the floor—and then ate it.

—MADI LEGERE

I'm not sure what's more confusing, that we would celebrate killing two birds or that we would need to conserve stones.

—@RCKRUSEKONTROL

i wonder if this will bounce
theycantclk.com
maybe that one will

The difference between dog people and cat people: Dog people wish their dogs were people. Cat people wish they were cats.

—@SIMONSINEK

We had recently installed a cat door on the back door of our house, but our four kitties couldn't figure out how to use it. Late one night, I heard a loud crunching and wondered which of the cats was eating at that hour. I got up to check, and there was a large possum by the cat bowl—it had come into the house through the cat door. When I startled the possum, the cats watched it leave—and by golly, they finally figured out the cat door. Thank you, Mr. Possum. Your work here is done.

—RUTH HOWDER

A snake slithers into a bar and the bartender says, "Sorry, buddy, but I can't serve you."

"Why not?" the snake asks.

"Because you can't hold your liquor."

—LYNDELL LEATHERMAN

My 17-year-old child forgot the word *foal* and called it a horse puppy instead.

—@BRAMPTONMEL

My favorite species of birds are the ones named by people who clearly hate birds.

- Drab seedeater
- Go-away bird
- Rough-faced shag
- Common loon
- Sad flycatcher
- Little bustard
- Perplexing scrubwren
- Satanic nightjar
- Monotonous lark

—@STU_BOT3000

"**We actually** get this question on a pretty regular basis," says an official with Iowa's Department of Transportation. The source of confusion: The deer-crossing signs that are posted along the road. And the question: "Why don't you put these signs where it's safer for the deer to cross?"

—KCRG.COM

I was shopping in the pet section of my local supermarket when I overheard a woman singing the praises of a particular water bowl to her husband.

"Look, it even has a water filter!" she said, holding the doggie dish out for her husband's inspection.

He had a slightly different take on things: "Dear, he drinks out of the toilet."

—JAMES JENKINS

A college girl was visiting my farm and noticed the ring in our bull's nose. Intrigued, she asked, "Did you put that ring in his nose, or was he born that way?"

—DONNA HATCH

My niece bought a hamster for her 5-year-old daughter, Kayleigh. One day it escaped from its cage. The family turned the house upside down and finally found the hamster. Several weeks later, while Kayleigh was at school, it escaped from the cage again. My niece searched frantically but never found the critter. Hoping to make the loss less painful for Kayleigh, my niece took the cage out of her room. When Kayleigh came home from school that afternoon, she climbed into her mother's lap.

"Mom, we've got a serious problem," she announced. "Not only is my hamster gone again, but this time it also took the cage."

—PATSY STRINGER

If you think dogs can't count, try putting three dog biscuits in your pocket and then giving Fido only two of them.

—PHIL PASTORET

The fact that we know chameleons exist means they are worthless idiot failures.

—@PEACHCOFFIN

TELEPATHY WITH ... MY DOG?

One pet owner struggles to see the world from a dog's eye view

By Patricia Pearson

y trouble with dogs is that I never have the remotest clue what they want, and they never seem to have the slightest inkling what I'm saying to them.

This domestic impasse became legendary in my family when we had a dog named Kevin. He was a cross between a border collie and a basenji, which means that half of him descended from the smartest breed and the other half from easily one of the stupidest. Kevin was highly alert, yet unable to grasp a single thing. His entire communicative repertoire—whether he wanted food, exercise, permission to jump on the sofa, a toy or, who knows, a conversation about the electric bill—consisted of padding up to me and staring. He did this about 50 times a day, just staring brightly without moving a muscle, and after years of living together I still didn't know what he wanted.

My husband would let Kevin stare at him until his eyeballs fell out and not worry about it. He took Kevin for walks, fed him and let him sleep on the bed. Done. But as a mother, I was wired to worry about how everyone was feeling.

So, one evening I left Kevin at home and, with about 20 other confused pet owners, attended a workshop led by a pet telepathist who I hoped would explain the trick to reading Kevin's mind. She arrived for the class carrying a slim gray cat named Moose, whom she introduced as her assistant. The cat soon shot into a closet, where he remained for the next two hours.

"Moose is going to be invisible for a while, but that will help you get used to communicating with pets at a distance," our instructor assured us, beaming. We nodded, awaiting a message from Moose, such as "Get me the hell out of here." In the meantime, our teacher explained what she knew about animal communication.

"The thing that animals want most in their life is to be heard," she said, sitting on a desk, "especially the birds. They really have a lot to say because they travel around the world." Um, what? "Don't analyze; don't edit," she warned, about receiving messages. "Just be willing to say, 'That was real.'"

She had us work in pairs. The woman beside me was to tune in to Kevin, who was at home sniffing about, and I was to pick up her cat's thoughts. We were both uncertain, but we'd paid our money. So I offered that her cat was ... under the bed ... and wanted to go out? She countered that Kevin was ... lying in front of the fireplace ... and also wanted to go out.

We reported our findings to the class, feeling like a pair of Pinocchios.

Back home, my husband suggested I contact the instructor for a personal consultation with Kevin. "Let them go mano a mano," Ambrose urged. "Just her and him." I couldn't resist.

When I introduced the telepathist to her subject, he was sound asleep and snoring on our dining room floor. I asked her what he was thinking.

"He says that you, as a family, should lighten up," she reported. Otherwise, she said, Kevin was happy with his role in life: to be a teacher to us, to help us connect with our energies and "to receive messages from him." *This is just a vicious circle,* I thought. *What messages?*

My husband interrupted: "Ask Kevin who killed our nephew's gerbil—him or Biscuit?" (Biscuit was my sister's golden retriever, who couldn't be in a room two seconds without knocking something over. She drove my sister bananas.)

Undaunted, the telepathist asked the deeply asleep Kevin if he was responsible for a certain tiny corpse appearing beneath my nephew's bed the previous summer. Then she looked at me. "Kevin says it was sad and it happened very fast, but his back was turned at the time." Upon hearing this, Ambrose had to go outside and bray with laughter.

Meanwhile, she offered to tune in to Biscuit, because maybe Kevin was evading responsibility. Moments later, she told us that yes, Biscuit had killed the gerbil, "and she's not sorry."

I thanked the pet telepathist and ran to call my sister at work. "BISCUIT DID IT—AND SHE'S NOT SORRY!" My sister fell off her chair laughing.

This became a widely shared tale in the family, so everyone is preparing to be amused by how I fare with our new pup—a 7-week-old Australian shepherd. This breed is one of the most energetic on the planet. I, on the other hand, am bookish, lazy and middle-aged. Never mind the dog—what was *I* thinking?

My son is an avid listener to our city's police frequency, and leaves the scanner on all the time. One morning while making his bed, I heard the dispatcher say, "Car 34, there is a 5-foot boa constrictor in a front yard. The resident wants a policeman to come and remove it." There was a long pause, then some static. Slowly, a voice said, "We can't start the car."

—JANET R. SMITH

My father and a friend were talking about the doors they had installed so their animals could let themselves in and out of the house. My dad asked his friend, who had two massive Great Danes, "Aren't you afraid that somebody might crawl through the dogs' door and steal something?"

"If you saw an opening that big," said his friend, "would you crawl through it?"

—HORST JENKINS

"**No, YOU** are a drama queen," said the fainting goat to the opossum.

—@_WATER_BABY

I was in the middle of grading my students' homework, and my husband and I decided we were hungry. So I left all the papers organized in neat piles, and we ducked out. I returned an hour later to discover that my puppy had found the papers. The next day, I called three of my students over to my desk to explain why I was giving them all a 100% grade on their assignments: "My dog ate your homework."

—JOANNE BEER

For my stepdaughter's 14th birthday, I had picked up a birthday card to be from the dog, in which I wrote numerous *woof*s and enclosed $50. I placed it by the front door, knowing Jessica would see it before leaving for school. In the morning, my fiancée, Denine, was driving Jessica and her younger sister, Olivia, to school when Jessica opened the card and read it out loud.

"Fifty dollars!" Olivia exclaimed. "I didn't think the dog even liked you that much!"

—DAREN WESTMAN

People freak out because of sharks in the ocean. News flash: That's where they live! If you see them at Chipotle, then we have a problem.

—@BIGKEFD

AM
HOUR OF RISING
WORM ACQUISITION
100
90
80
70
60
50
40
30
20
10
0
HMMMM...

My neighbor's son picked up a stray dog and named it Sam. Some time later, I was having coffee at their house and inquired about Sam.

"Oh, the dog is fine," my neighbor said. "She had a litter of puppies, and so we fixed the problem. Now we call her Sam Spayed."

—JUDY CHRISTENSEN

Quick Quips

Whoever named the ewe really didn't like female sheep.

—@DAWN_MAESTAS

The worst part about being a giraffe is having a lot of time to think about your mistakes when you're sinking into quicksand.

—@ROLLDIGGITY

Ant: a small insect that, though always at work, still finds time to go to picnics.

—ANONYMOUS

What do you call a lazy baby kangaroo? *A pouch potato.*

—JACOB SCHOLL

If bees made beer, we would be taking better care of them.

—BLORE40 ON REDDIT.COM

Interesting fact: A shark will attack you only if you're wet.

—SEAN LOCK

When cats are sad:

Bartender: What'll ya have?

Cat: Shot of rum.

[Bartender pours it.]

[Cat slowly pushes it off the bar.]

Cat: Another.

—@PHILJAMESSON

Shipwreck Diary

Day 1: Alone, doing well. Mentally sound. Met a crab.

Day 2: I have married the crab.

Day 3: I have eaten my wife.

—@MURRMAN5

My husband walked into the room and said, "How's my sleeping beauty?" I smiled and opened my eyes just in time to see him pat my sleeping puppy's head.

—@VISIONBORED1

One afternoon my 6-year-old daughter showed me a picture of a fat cat she had drawn. I asked her what kind it was and she told me it was a cat that was going to have kittens.

"See, I'll show you," she said. Carefully, she outlined in pencil four very small kittens inside the cat's body.

I then asked, "And do you know how they got there?"

Looking at me seriously, she said, "Of course I know. I drew them!"

—LINDA CLARK

A fellow salesperson, an animal lover, was suddenly overcome by allergies at one of our company meetings. Coughing, sniffling, watery eyes ... she was a mess.

"If you have such terrible allergies, why do you keep so many pets?" asked a friend.

"Because"—*sneeze, cough, hack*—"if I'm going to be sick, I might as well have company."

—JOHN CALDWELL

Giraffes were invented in 1780 when three horses accidentally swallowed a ladder.

—@KIMMYMONTE

The chihuahua at my vet's office was quiet right up until a huge Rottweiler came in. Suddenly, the 6-pounder became Cujo—barking and slavering.

"Oh please," said its owner. "The only way you could hurt that dog would be if you got stuck in his throat."

—LINDA MARTIN

Snake 1: Are we poisonous?

Snake 2: I don't know. Why?

Snake 1: I just bit my lip.

—FAITH LACKEY

Young Billy and Willy were walking home from Sunday school, where they had just learned about Noah's ark. Willy asked, "Do you think Noah did much fishing?"

"How could he?" said Billy. "He had only two worms."

—THEADVOCATE.COM

A Pennsylvania man plagued by opossums in his yard set fire to a pile of leaves, hoping to scare off the marsupials. We don't know whether it worked, but he did succeed in nearly burning down his home, causing $50,000 worth of damage.

—CBSNEWS.COM

Sometimes I like to sit my dog down for a performance review, just to remind him who's boss.

—@RMFNORD

QUOTABLE QUOTES

I CAN TELL YOU THAT I'D RATHER BE KISSED BY MY DOGS THAN BY SOME PEOPLE I'VE KNOWN.

—BOB BARKER

Turkeys are peacocks that have let themselves go.

—KRISTEN SCHAAL

Never get between a female grizzly and one of her young, particularly if he's just told her that he intends to drop out of college to focus on his band.

—ANDY G. IHNATKO

I believe implicitly that every young man in the world is fascinated with either sharks or dinosaurs.

—ROBERT BENCHLEY

Ever wonder what pets must think of us? I mean, here we come back from a grocery store with the most amazing haul—chicken, pork, half a cow. They must think we're the greatest hunters on earth!

—ANNE TYLER

To be or not to be a horse rider, that is equestrian.

—MARK SIMMONS

If a dog jumps in your lap, it is because he is fond of you, but if a cat does the same thing, it is because your lap is warmer.

—ALFRED NORTH WHITEHEAD

Our perfect companions never have fewer than four feet.

—COLETTE

I have lived with several Zen masters—all of them cats.

—ECKHART TOLLE

NOTHING IS MADE IN VAIN, BUT THE FLY CAME NEAR IT.

—MARK TWAIN

AIM HIGH

Using a BB gun on a mouse might be the definition of overshooting

By Melody Durant

Years ago we lived in a beautiful parsonage that sat on a hill above the neighboring catfish farms. It was a lovely house, but it was not quite as tight as we might have hoped.

Neighbors would often ask if we knew that when the house was built, a rattlesnake had found its way in. And then, several years later, we came home to find a snakeskin at the front door—but we never found its owner.

One winter it seemed all the local mice had chosen our home to move their families into. We do try to make everyone feel comfortable when they come to visit, but really—a herd of mice was too much.

I was on the phone with my brother-in-law one day soon after we became aware of the invasion, and as I leaned against the kitchen counter, I noticed a mouse just strutting its way across my kitchen floor—taking its time and seemingly in no hurry at all.

I told my brother-in-law I needed to go—I had to shoot a mouse in the house. "Don't hurt the kids!" I could hear him saying as I hung up the phone.

Determined to see my plan through, I grabbed my son's BB gun. It had an attached scope, which I peered through to slowly pinpoint Mr. Mouse under the table. I pulled the trigger, and down went the mouse! By my kids' reaction, you would have thought I had saved them from a charging tiger.

Not long after, my mom called, and I told her about the excitement in the kitchen. Mom is a demure woman, and she suggested I not tell anyone, lest I bring attention to myself. *Sure, Mom*, I thought. *I just shot a mouse in the house and you don't want me to tell anyone?* No way. This should become a family legend.

CHILD'S PLAY

My wife was dismayed when my sister told us that our 2-year-old nephew was constantly asking to see me and never mentioning her. She could not figure out why a toddler would prefer his Uncle Chris (me) to his Aunt Crissy (her). I basked in my status as the favorite until the next time we saw him, when, with arms wide open, he ran right past me and to my wife, shouting, "Uncle Chris! Uncle Chris!"

—CHRIS YODICE

I was driving with my young twin grandsons when their mother called. As we chatted over the car's Bluetooth speaker, one of the boys yelled out from the back, "Hey, Mom, guess who this is? Is it me or Luke?"

After a slight pause, the boys' mother remarked, "And he's the smart one."

—MARY MEILLIER

This morning I brushed my hair with an American Girl doll brush because apparently she's the only one in my house who puts things back where they belong.

—@MOMMAJESSIEC

When my neighbor's granddaughter introduced me to her young son, Brian, I said to him, "My grandchildren call me Mimi. Why don't you call me that too?"

"I don't think so," he retorted, and ran off after his mother.

A few weeks later I was asked to babysit for Brian, and we hit it off wonderfully. As he snuggled up next to me, he said, "I don't care what your grandchildren say. I love you, Meanie."

—MARILYN HAYDEN

Whenever my 3-year-old grandson comes to visit, we inevitably play Army. I'm the lowly private, and he's the general barking out orders: "Soldier, do this! Soldier, do that!" One day, while we were playing, he needed to use the bathroom. A few minutes later, the door opened and there he stood, his pants around his ankles, shouting, "Soldier! I can't get my pants up!"

—KATHY DEVER

I was taking a shower when my 3-year-old granddaughter walked in on me in all my glory. "Grandma," she said, stunned, "you don't have your glasses on."

—ALICE HORNE

"Seriously ... how well do we really know Mom?"

Our 6-year-old daughter, Terra, has a need to ask questions ... lots of questions. Finally, one day, my wife had had it.

"Have you ever heard that curiosity killed the cat?" my wife asked.

"No," replied Terra.

"Well, there was a cat, and he was very inquisitive. And one day, he looked into a big hole, fell in and died!"

Terra was intrigued: "What was in the hole?"

—HECTOR BERNASCONI

There's going to be a point in my life when my son looks up at me and thinks, "Gee, my mom knows everything!"

Then he'll get to sixth grade math class, and I'll say, "Well, kid, this is where we part ways."

—@HANNAHEINBINDER

While my 3-year-old grandson was attending a birthday party, his friend's father sneaked off to take a shower before work. Halfway through, the father heard a tapping on the shower door, followed by the sight of my grandson peering in. Looking around the stall, he asked, "Is my mom in here?"

—BILLIE CREEL

"I downloaded the parental control app, but they're still not doing what I want them to do."

I was not thrilled with the idea of letting my clueless 13-year-old son babysit his younger sisters, even though he begged me to.

"What about a fire?" I asked, referring to my No. 1 concern.

"Mom," he said, rolling his eyes, "I'm a Boy Scout. I know how to start a fire."

—JO WALKER

I overheard my 7-year-old son and his friends discussing the tooth fairy, the Easter Bunny and Santa Claus. "Steven says it's the parents who bring the toys," he said skeptically, "but I know my parents wouldn't know how to drive the reindeer."

—SHARON PRICE

My toddler just spent five minutes explaining that he can't use his imagination because he traded it to a kid at day care for some fruit snacks.

—@HENPECKEDHAL

When my 8-year-old sister came to visit, I took a day off from my job at the Pentagon and showed her the Lincoln Memorial. There, etched into the monument, she saw a large block of text—272 words long.

"What is that?" she asked.

"It's Lincoln's Gettysburg Address," I told her.

"If that is his address, how does he get any mail?"

—DANIEL PALOMO

Potty Training

In case you were wondering, the loudest sound in the world is my kid screaming "Are you pooping?!?" in a public restroom.

—@UNFILTEREDMAMA

My kids always perceived the bathroom as a place where you wait it out until all the groceries are unloaded from the car.

—ERMA BOMBECK

I was working from home, interviewing a famous neurologist for an article, when my 3-year-old announced she had to go potty and waddled into the bathroom. After some loud moans, she yelled, "I did it, Mom! I pooped in the toilet! I pooped on the floor too! But I'll clean it! Oh, I stepped in it!"

There was an uncomfortable silence as I realized the doctor had heard every word.

"Ha ha," I laughed nervously. "Do you have kids?"

"No," he said, "and I never will."

—CHARLOTTE ANDERSEN

The morning that he began kindergarten, I told my son about the great adventure that awaited him at school.

"You're going to learn so many things," I said, "like how to read and write!"

When I picked him up later that afternoon, I asked how it went.

"Well," he said, "I still can't read or write."

—DEBBIE CRISS

I'm teaching my kids to read to help them succeed in school. I'm teaching my kids to read because it's quality time spent together. But most of all I'm teaching my kids to read so they won't ask "What does XJ49PB2 spell?" every time we pass another car on the road.

—@HENPECKEDHAL

Things you will never hear a 3-year-old say:

- "It doesn't really look like a dragon, but never mind, I'll eat it anyway—food is food!"
- "Don't hide that square millimeter of zucchini behind the pasta. More! More green! I'm into microsprouts at the moment too."
- "Yep, that's exactly how I wanted it done. You've nailed it. Again."
- "I don't need it. I already have three. Let's just stick to our shopping list."
- "For Pete's sake, Dad. It's 3:30 in the morning. Please, go back to bed—you're starting a new job, and this is the one night you really need some decent sleep."
- "It doesn't matter how we did this yesterday. Things change!"
- "Here is the remote—I don't really know how to use it anyway."
- "I bet I can get in my car seat before you can say the words 'My back. I can't ... straighten ... up ...'"
- "Here's your phone back."

—OLIVIA APPLEBY ON MCSWEENEYS.NET

All the baby books tell you that infants need to eat every two to three hours, but what they fail to mention is that this behavior continues until the child turns 18 and moves out of your house.

—@MOMTRUTHBOMB

My husband is helping me relax by taking the kids to school this morning. We went over the drop-off procedure 37 times and he just left without the kids.

—@MARYFAIRYBOBRRY

PARENTING: TO CODDLE OR NEGLECT?

While praise and pampering are heaped upon the firstborn, younger siblings tend to play second fiddle

By Richard Glover

The youngest sibling in a family, according to a recent report, is often sleeker and fitter than the first-born child. While I'm with the scientists when it comes to global warming, the importance of vaccines and the need for dental hygiene, I feel compelled to break ranks on this assessment.

I have had children of my own, and I have observed the children of others. The only possible conclusion is this: Standards slip with each additional child.

With the firstborn, everything must be perfect. They are fed a balanced diet of high-quality vegetables and organically reared meat. The staff, by which I mean the mother and father, are in the kitchen night and day, pausing in their culinary efforts only to read linguistically challenging texts and to perform interpretative global folk dances for the child's amusement.

Photographs are taken, almost constantly, recording events such as First Burp, First Wriggle and What We Took to Be the First Smile but in Retrospect Was Just Colic.

As the child grows older, a loving, protective and educationally rich system is established in which the child is permitted to watch one hour of television each week, providing it's a nature documentary.

Ballet shoes are purchased. A cello—a cello!—is not considered too great an expense. The first soccer game is witnessed not by one parent, but by two parents, four grandparents and an uncle visiting from overseas. There are pop stars with smaller entourages.

The child, inevitably, is considered "gifted."

> ***The number of photographs moderates from five a day to one every six weeks.***

It's at this point that the second child is born. Standards immediately decline.

The hand-operated mincer, in which baby food had previously been freshly prepared each day by the kitchen staff, is never retrieved from the bottom drawer. Instead, commercially produced slop is suddenly considered "nutritionally superior—and so much more convenient." The bedtime reading session, which, with the first child, had involved 50 minutes of funny voices and entertaining asides, now lasts the three minutes between when Daddy first lies on the bed and when Daddy begins snoring.

The number of photographs moderates from five a day to one every six weeks. A trendy brand of jumpsuits in which the first child was dressed have been replaced with cheap copies from the discount store around the corner.

Television viewing is still restricted to "nature documentaries," but the definition of nature documentaries appears to have widened to include *The Lion King*, *Toy Story 4*, and real-estate reality shows.

The soccer entourage has dwindled to one rather hungover father, whose interest seems to be largely focused on finding something to eat. And the request for a trumpet, in order to join the school band, is declined on the basis of expense—why don't you try Mom's old guitar?

All this, of course, is just limbering up for the arrival of the third child, at which point standards collapse completely.

The definition of toddler food has now grown to include a serving of nachos and some gnawing on the edge of last night's pizza. This "meal" is served while watching a nature documentary—one that appears to involve Bruce Willis shooting at people in a New York airport.

The third child will be 6 years old before they are the subject of a single photograph, and even then it's just their right leg in a photo of the dog. They are dressed in clothes handed down from a second cousin, soaked in extra-strength detergent to remove the stains.

They hitchhike to soccer.

They learn music on a kazoo.

When it comes to table manners, the only guidance they are given involves the phrase: "Don't wipe your hands on the furniture, that's disgusting. Use your T-shirt like your father does."

How, given all of this, can science still claim that the youngest siblings tend to be the healthiest?

Their theory, should you be interested, goes like this: First-time mothers, it is said, are less adept at pumping calories into the kid when the kid is still in the womb, and so the proto-kid shifts its metabolism in order to store more fat.

This then becomes a lifetime habit, with the firstborns waddling around trying to keep up with their sleeker, younger siblings.

What nonsense. Here's my alternative theory: The younger ones, having grown up with parents oblivious to their welfare, are now living a life so dissolute they don't have time to put on weight.

Offer them a home-cooked meal and they'll decline—they'd rather go outside and smoke a cigarette.

Or maybe, just maybe, humans are like grapevines. The best wine often comes from grapes planted in stony soil and starved of water. They thrive on the neglect. The grapes are smaller but more powerful, filled with flavor. And that may be the story of the fit, slim and intense younger siblings.

I'd like to prove my various theories by showing you a few photographs of these later-born children, recording the circumstances of their childhood and adolescence. What a shame that there appear to be none in existence.

THE KIDS ARE ASLEEP. LET'S GO TO EUROPE.
MUELLER

Friends of ours were just finishing their dinner on a late-spring evening when suddenly they heard the chimes of the first ice cream truck of the season. Their 9-year-old son jumped up from the table and raced to the front door, hollering to his sister: "I'll go stop the truck! You stay here and beg."

—IRENE SWANTON

After my 10-year-old daughter declared her disgust with cosmetic surgery, I dropped a bomb on her.

"Don't be too quick to judge," I told her. "Before college, I had a nose job." She was completely thrown.

"You mean," she said, "it was bigger?"

—TANYA SCHERSCHEL

After learning her friend had broken his arm, my 5-year-old daughter insisted on drawing him a picture. She sat at the table for an hour, coloring carefully, then handed me a piece of paper.

"It's very pretty," I said. "I bet this will make him feel better."

She smiled. "And I wrote him a letter on the back."

"Oh!" I turned the paper over to look at the back, which was covered in random letters and scribbles. "Um ... what does it say?"

She just shrugged. "How would I know?" she said. "I can't read."

—KATIE POWNER

Life hack for parents: Convince your kids you hate something you actually like. My 5- and 7-year-olds just spent 10 minutes "tormenting" me by massaging my shoulders.

—@LEXMOBILEGAMING

Following multiple failed attempts to sleep in my bed, my 3-year-old came creeping in wearing sunglasses. After being denied once again, she said, "I tried a disguise this time. I thought for sure it would work."

—@_SINGLEBABYMAMA

When my 5-year-old came home from his very first day in kindergarten, I excitedly asked, "So how was your first day of school?"

Dropping his backpack, he said, "Well, I'll tell you one thing: I am never going back to that place."

—KAY MARSKE

My 3-year-old said she wanted to be an astronaut, and I said she had to study hard, go to college, learn a lot of science and take a physical fitness test. She shrugged and said, "That's just four things."

—@JENDZIURA

Most parents lie to their kids at some point, but these whoppers are in a league of their own:

- We got our daughter to eat fish by calling it Argentinian chicken.
- "If the ice cream truck is playing music, it means it has run out of ice cream."
- Our parents used to tell my only brother and me that we used to have another brother who turned into a mushroom from not taking a bath. They even added him to the family albums.
- My dad said if I looked after a special growing rock and watered it each day until it stopped growing, I could get a dog. I'd water the rock, and every week, while I was at school, he'd replace it with a slightly bigger rock.
- When I was little, my dad told me that toys grew under the weeds in the yard and that if I pulled them, eventually a toy would pop out. And I believed it!
- "They don't sell replacement batteries for that toy."

—BOREDPANDA.COM AND REDDIT.COM

"Go ask your mother."

DO LOOK BEHIND THAT CURTAIN

A sister's shower stunt dripped with irony

By Janet Ingram

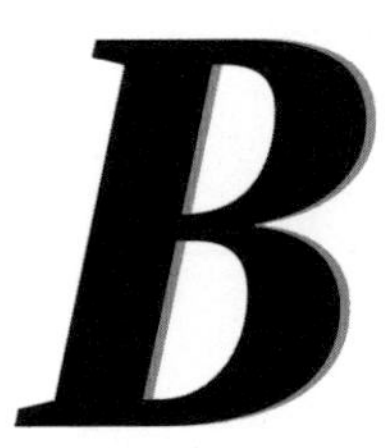

ack in 1965, when I was 13, I came home from a babysitting job to an empty house. My parents and brother were at church, and my sister was at work. I decided to take a shower, so I went into the bathroom and peeled off my clothes. Just then, I heard my sister come home. I decided this was the perfect opportunity to scare her, so I hid behind the shower curtain to lunge out when she passed by. But instead of coming in, she dropped everything and ran out the door. *Sheesh! What's wrong with her?* I wondered. I shrugged it off and took my shower.

Unfortunately, I was in for a nasty shock of my own. Without realizing it, I had frightened my sister: She'd heard the shower curtain rustling, seen my clothes and thought the worst. She had jumped back into her car, sped to church and burst into the service shouting, "There's someone in the house, and I saw Janet's clothes on the floor!" My family bolted from the church, believing that something terrible had happened to me. Dad was speeding, so a cop pulled him over. After Dad told him the situation, the police officer followed him home.

The next thing I knew, my entire family and the policeman were running in to see if I was OK. I was forced to explain to everyone that there had been no intruder, I'd just been hiding in the shower to scare my sister. Talk about embarrassing. To make matters worse, everyone from church dropped by later that evening, one by painful one, to make sure I was all right.

That was the first—and last—time I ever tried to pull a prank on my excitable older sister.

DAD!
DAD!
DAD!!
I'M COMING!
I'M COMING!
WHAT IS IT?!!
WE
LOST
OUR
SIGNAL.
Hagen

I accidentally threw away my 4-year-old's favorite candy wrapper. Please keep us both in your thoughts during this difficult time.

—@AKNOTT21

At a gymnastics "competition," my 3-year-old was posing with her trophy. Suddenly, she tripped. The trophy crashed, breaking in half. Everyone gasped, expecting tears. She picked it up and said, "Look! Now I have two trophies!"

—@MARVINALLEN

After a typical rapid-fire question session with our 5-year-old, my wife wondered out loud why she asks so many questions. Her response: "Well, I don't know anything."

—REDDIT.COM

On a demographics survey given at our high school, students were asked, "What disadvantages do you see in having children?" Usual answers included "It's expensive to raise kids" and "They take up a lot of your time." But one boy was not worried about money or responsibility. He wrote, "If I have children, I might have to drive a minivan."

—CHERITH DIEMERT

Today, a first grader told me that she doesn't need to learn what I'm teaching because she wants to be a pineapple when she grows up.

—@TEACHERONTOPIC

When our school librarian announced she was changing schools, my fellow teacher asked a student, "Why do you think Ms. Richardson is leaving?"

The third grader opined, "Because she's read all of our books?"

—SCOTT MUIR

When I asked my 5-year-old grandson why he was so anxious to turn 6, he replied, "So I can finally get married and have kids!"

—JULEE SMITH

Dubious claims my toddler made this week:

- He invented the thumbs-up.
- Only "some" lizards can read.
- He forgot how to eat carrots.
- His day care allows swords.

—@HENPECKEDHAL

Wife: "The Romans were gluttons. They overdid everything."

Daughter, age 11: "You can't overdo water parks."

—@ROBCORDDRY

QUOTABLE QUOTES

RAISING KIDS MAY BE A THANKLESS JOB WITH RIDICULOUS HOURS, BUT AT LEAST THE PAY SUCKS.

—JIM GAFFIGAN

Adults are always asking children what they want to be when they grow up ... they're looking for ideas.

—PAULA POUNDSTONE

Having a family is like having a bowling alley installed in your brain.

—MARTIN MULL

Babies are such a nice way to start people.

—DON HEROLD

Remember: What Dad really wants is a nap. Really.

—DAVE BARRY

Setting a good example for your children does nothing but increase their embarrassment.

—DOUG LARSON

Youth is a wonderful thing. What a crime to waste it on children.

—GEORGE BERNARD SHAW

My wife is so analytical with raising kids, and I am not. My feeling is if they turn out good, then that means I was a good daddy and put a lot of effort into it. If they turn out bad, it means they took after her side of the family.

—JEFF FOXWORTHY

I've been to war. I've raised twins. If I had a choice, I'd rather go to war.

—GEORGE W. BUSH

Motherhood is not for the fainthearted. Frogs, skinned knees and the insults of teenage girls are not meant for the wimpy.

—DANIELLE STEELE

BEING A DAD IS THE GREATEST, EXCEPT FOR ASSEMBLING THINGS.

—CONAN O'BRIEN

A COOKED-UP SCHEME FALLS FLAT

He'd soon be eating his words, along with the cake

By Paul Kieffer

big chocolate cake should be all it takes to make a 10-year-old boy happy on his birthday. But one cake turned out to be food for thought that has lasted a lifetime.

On the morning of my birthday, June 2, my mother ordered a chocolate cake from our neighborhood bakery. She asked my friend and me to pick it up and told us to walk there, but we rode our bikes instead—big mistake.

As we rode to the bakery, we were having fun tossing a ball back and forth between us. We could easily ride no-handed—without holding onto the handlebars.

We picked up the cake and resumed our game of catch as we rode home. I had the cake balanced in one hand and was playing catch with the other. All was going well until I hit a bump—and, of course, I dropped my cake.

Being a quick thinker, I came up with a perfectly believable story: I told my mother that the lady at the bakery must have handed me the box upside down, causing the icing to be messed up. My wise mother knew I was lying, but instead of losing her temper, she devised an ingenious plan that put the dilemma back where it belonged—with me.

She told me to return to the store and tell the woman that she'd handed me my cake upside down. *Now what was I going to do? I'd be caught in my lie.*

So back to the bakery I went—alone since my friend had deserted me in my hour of need. There, I informed the baker what she had done. She just smiled and said she'd re-ice the cake if I promised to confess the truth to my mother.

Still now, whenever I eat chocolate cake, I recall my mother's piece of wisdom about telling lies.

4

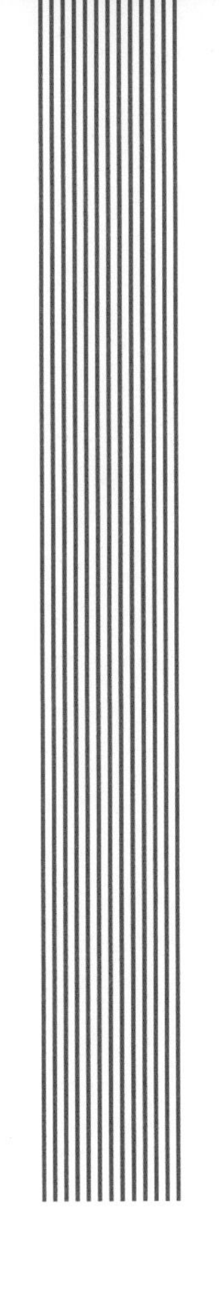

STAGES, PAGES & SCREENS

We invited another couple to be our guests at a Metropolitan Opera performance of *Othello*. Since they were unfamiliar with the opera, I spent the taxi ride to the theater unraveling the plot for them. The cab's arrival at the Met coincided with my recounting of the climax. Before finishing, I handed over the fare to the driver and prepared to get out.

"Stop!" demanded the driver. "No one is leaving until I hear the end."

—VERN SCHRAMM

While doing volunteer work, I began to sing a favorite song of mine to pass the time. Another volunteer perked his ears.

"Who sings that?" he asked.

"The Traveling Wilburys," I replied.

He nodded. "Well, let's keep it that way."

—CHRISTOPHER THORSEN

New and improved book titles to make the classics less stuffy:

- *How I Met Your Mother* (replaces *Oedipus the King*)
- *There Will Be Blood* (replaces *What to Expect When You're Expecting*)
- *A Bug's Life* (replaces *The Metamorphosis*)

—DAN WILBUR IN *NEVER FLIRT WITH PUPPY KILLERS*

Before Willie Nelson's longtime harmonica player, Mickey Raphael, officially joined the band, he'd show up at gigs and just start playing. After a while, Willie got confused.

"One day, Willie asked Paul English, his drummer, 'What are we paying Mickey?' And Paul goes, 'Nothing; he's just coming to sit in.' Willie replies, 'Well, double his salary.'"

—*TEXAS MONTHLY*

Years ago, a children's book was published detailing the mischievous behavior of young John Hancock, Paul Revere, George Washington and Ben Franklin. One day, a customer walked into our library and read the book's title: *John, Paul, George & Ben*. With a look of abject confusion, she said, "I didn't know Ringo's real name was Ben."

—JOANN MEADOWS

I'm gonna write a book about the difficulties of watching *Pride and Prejudice* dubbed into French. It will be called *L'Austen Translation*.

—@GREG_JENNER

A Hollywood producer calls his friend, another Hollywood producer, on the phone.

"Hey, how are you doing?" he asks.

"Well!" responds the friend. "I just sold a screenplay for $200,000. I also wrote a new novel and got a $50,000 advance from the publisher. I have a new TV series airing next week, and everyone says it's going to be a hit. I'm doing great! How are you?"

"OK," says the first producer. "I'll call back when you're alone."

—JIM PIETSCH IN *THE NEW YORK CITY CAB DRIVER'S JOKE BOOK*

Mom, who is 94 and an avid reader, was perusing a list of new books from the public library when she noted, disappointedly, "I never see familiar authors on these lists."

My ever-helpful husband explained, "That's because Louisa May Alcott died."

—COLLEEN WEBER

My question is this: Did Disney come up with the movie and then the name, or did someone just think of the pun *aristocats* and design the entire movie around it?

—@MEMANTULA

Italian artist Salvatore Garau created an artwork that must be seen to believed. Only, you can't see it. It's invisible. Still, that didn't stop Garau from successfully selling the nonexistent artwork to someone for $18,300. The new owner went home with very real instructions: The work, which is, to repeat, invisible, must be displayed in a five-by-five-foot space free of obstruction.

—ARTNET.COM

While my friend and I were waiting in the Ritz-Carlton lobby, we spotted opera great Andrea Bocelli. My friend was so excited. He ran up to Mr. Bocelli, grabbed his hand and started pumping it vigorously, while proclaiming, "I am a huge fan of yours, Mr. Pavarotti!" Thankfully, Mr. Bocelli saw the humor.

—DEB WEIDENHAMER

Meet the most absurd Hollywood cliches Twitter has to offer:

- Hello. I am a person using a phone in a movie. I don't say goodbye before I hang up. I just stop talking and put the phone down and the person on the other end somehow just knows I'm not there anymore.

—@MATTSINGER

- Hello. I'm a bar patron in a movie. I can walk into any bar for the first time and say "Two beers, please" and the bartender will hand me two beers with no discussion of type, brand or receptacle.

—@TJCHAMBERSLA

- Hello. I'm a nurse in a movie. I sit at a desk and know nothing but visiting hours and the location of every patient and doctor in the hospital.

—@POLITINURSE

- Hi. I'm the best friend of a murder victim. Even though the police come to my workplace to question me about my dead friend, I'll just unload this truck or clear these busy tables as we talk instead of giving them my full attention.

—@STEVE_EIFERT

- Hello. I'm the Golden Gate Bridge in a movie. I will be destroyed.

—@MICHAELLEVYSF

I feel strongly that the visual arts are of vast importance. Of course I could be prejudiced.I am a visual art.

—KERMIT THE FROG

I would love for one second of my adult life to feel as amped as I did as a child knowing I had five bucks to spend at the Scholastic Book Fair.

—@KRISTEN_ARNETT

There's this story about a guy who was hanging around the circus, watching another guy picking up elephant dung and moving it over into a pile. It was hot and sweaty work, but he would go back and pick up another pile, then another pile. Finally the first guy said, "Man, why don't you get a real job?" And the elephant-dung guy said, "What, and quit show business?"

—WILLIE NELSON, WHEN ASKED ON NPR WHAT KEEPS HIM PERFORMING AT AGE 85

"Doc, I can't stop singing 'Green, Green Grass of Home.'"

"That sounds like Tom Jones syndrome."

"Is it common?"

"It's not unusual."

—GRUNTDOC.COM

A musician friend is always upbeat. But when she developed ringing in one ear, I was concerned it might overwhelm even her. When I asked whether her condition was especially annoying to a musician, she shook her head.

"Not really," she said cheerfully. "The ringing is in the key of B flat, so I use it to tune my cello half a tone lower."

—KATHLEEN CAHILL

Quick Quips

If I worked in a used-record store, I'd tell every customer that "all sales are vinyl."

—@WOODYLUVSCOFFEE

"They just got engaged but there are 200 pages left, so it's not looking good." —My daughter, on *Jane Eyre*

—@EILEENCURTRIGHT

Disney sets painfully unrealistic expectations. No dogs will eat my spaghetti.

—@ALLIEGOERTZ

Did the person who invented the phrase "one-hit wonder" invent any other popular phrases?

—@HONEYCUTTART

I don't get it.
Type the characters into the box below.
Blazek

There's not a whole lot to relieve the boredom when working in Antarctica, so books take on added importance. Too much importance, evidently. A Russian electrical engineer was once arrested for assaulting a co-worker. The reason behind the attack: His colleague kept ruining the endings of the books he was reading.

—VICE.COM

A chicken just told me her top three favorite composers of all time: Bach, Bach, Bach.

—@ERICDADOURIAN

Behold! Intentionally bad first lines to nonexistent novels, from the annual Bulwer-Lytton Fiction Contest.

- As Lewiston Creol plummeted down the sheer icy cliff, he pondered on the word *plummet*, but his pondering was interrupted by the surface of the water, at which point he ceased to plummet and began to plunge.

—JASON CHANDLER

- Baking under the blazing New Mexico sun as he stood in the dusty street outside the saloon, Old West certified public accountant Arthur W. Fetterman Jr. hovered his sweaty hand over the butt of his borrowed six-gun, advanced another reluctant step toward famed gunfighter John Wesley Hardin and wondered for the hundredth time what had possessed him to correct the man's use of "supposably" during their poker game.

—BILL WHITE

- She was the most desired object in the room, not unlike the last deviled egg at an Easter Day potluck.

—CHRISTINE HAMILTON

- Sven, who rode his unicycle while training for the biathlon, thought the triceratops was the most regal of dinosaurs, exercised in the quad of his apartment complex down the street from the Pentagon, sang in a sextet, had a deviated septum, fought for fun in a UFC octagon, seemed to have nine lives and spent a decade with Aboriginal people, was a man you could count on.

—JEFF GREEN

If teenage Mary Shelley can win a storytelling contest with Lord Byron by inventing science fiction, I can surely make it to Friday.

—@SKETCHESBYBOZE

My Netflix viewing history is just a list of movies I've fallen asleep to.

—@BOURGEOISALIEN

FUNNY, YOU DON'T LOOK LIKE DANIEL CRAIG

Sharing a name with a celebrity can be a blessing ... or a curse

By **Lenore Skenazy**

im Hoover, a new father, giddily filled in his son's birth certificate with the name of his old dog: Herbert. Then he asked the nurse for a new certificate.

"Only," she replied, "if you have another child."

Thus, a new Herbert Hoover came into the world in 1968, unintentionally honoring the president who ushered in the Great Depression. Herbert now lives in Harlem and makes pewter saltines (yes, you read that right) that are sold across the country.

So what were you expecting? A politician? A Republican, at least? After interviewing everyone from (not the) Michael Jordan to (not the) Michael Jackson—not to mention (not the) Betsy Ross, Oprah and a lot more—I've learned that very few of them would be mistaken for their famous namesakes. But they all feel connected to their celebrity counterparts, for better or worse (for Charles Manson, just worse). And if you happen to share a famous name, I suggest you be prepared for anything.

PERKS

Marcia Clark—the budding publicist, not the ex-prosecutor—moved to New York on the cusp of the O.J. Simpson trial, when her namesake in California was busy trying to convict the former NFL star of a double murder. "I'd get all these emails," the arts consultant says. "'Talk to the dog! The dog has all the information.'"

The only one who didn't pay her any special attention was her new boss—until the boss couldn't get reservations at a hot new restaurant. "Marcia," she said, "would you call and make a reservation for four in your name?"

A phone call later, a table was reserved for 1 o'clock that very afternoon. Too bad her boss didn't take Marcia along.

Hard-to-get reservations, upgrades, first-class tickets—a lot of folks with famous names enjoy them all. Dallas sales rep Carlos Santana got special treatment in first class because the flight attendant thought he was the musician's son. (Nope!) Same thing happened to marketing consultant Winton Churchill. Guess the airline didn't notice the missing *s* in his first name. (He was named for a car, not the late British prime minister.) When Detroit property manager James Joyce visits any of the many pubs that share his name, "It's usually good for a few free beers," he says. (By the way, this Joyce is a former teacher—and even he didn't make it through *Ulysses*.)

Expecting similar hospitality, a Californian John Hancock visited the Chicago skyscraper bearing his name. Arriving at the observatory, 94 floors up, he handed over his ID and asked with a twinkle in his eye, "Can I get in free?" Answer: No.

PAINS

Sharing a famous name is clearly not all upgrades and champagne. In fact, sometimes the champagne stops flowing pretty abruptly.

Businessman Brian Williams arrived at his Las Vegas hotel and was ushered into a fabulous suite. Less than an hour later, he was ushered out, with a brief apology.

"I was placed in a room on a lower floor, overlooking a water show," Williams says, only to hear "I'm proud to be an American" every 15 minutes.

When a car service was dispatched to pick up David Cassidy from the airport, the driver found himself chauffeuring a Long Island lawyer, not the *Partridge Family* singing sensation. "I told my wife I was picking up David Cassidy," said the driver.

"Well, you did!" replied the good-natured attorney.

"You know what I mean," the driver grumbled. Yes, indeed.

Communications expert Daniel Craig gamely explains to surprised receptionists, cashiers and clerks handling his credit card that he deliberately dropped the British accent, the tan and the six-pack abs "so I can blend in with all you regular people." How very James Bond of him.

Ted Kennedy, the head of CEO Challenges, a Colorado company that organizes networking events for captains of industry, has also tried charming people out of their disappointment. "I had a meeting with the city of Boston about a CEO cycling event, and it was absolutely packed to the rafters." Then Kennedy got up to introduce himself—and 90% of the people left. "I was like, 'Hey! Where are you all going? I'm as exciting as that other guy!' "

If ever he starts to feel sorry for himself, Kennedy recalls another noncelebrity celebrity encounter he had. "I met a guy named Ronald McDonald. I said, 'Oh, my God, I can't imagine what you go through!' He just shook his head, 'Yeah. It really sucks.' "

Nor is it a picnic being a 5-foot, 6-inch Michael Jordan. When the Atlanta editor of Thrillist arrived at an invitation-only party and announced, "I'm Michael Jordan," the three women at the check-in desk did a double take. Their smiles slid off. They demanded to see his license.

"It looks like you have a fake ID," sneered the most brazen one, bending the license back and forth.

Jordan politely requested they summon one of the party organizers. The organizer vouched for him, and the checker apologized. "She was really hoping to meet Michael Jordan that night and everyone was sad he wasn't coming," recalls the editor. "Then she asked for my autograph."

SUDDEN FAME

Some are born almost famous, some achieve almost-famousness and some have almost-famousness thrust upon them, as did one mother of four. It started slowly. A call or two a week. Usually something like, "Hi! It's Laura from high school! Remember me?"

Perplexed, the woman had to admit that no, she did not. "Sorry, you have the wrong number."

"This is how Kelly Clarkson learned of a new show called American Idol."

"You're lying!" cried the caller before slamming down the phone. Similar calls grew in number each week. Old ladies. Young girls. Drunk frat guys. This is how Kelly Clarkson learned of a new show called *American Idol.*

"The calls became more and more frequent, and the night she won, the phone was ringing off the hook," recalls Clarkson, who, like the "Because of You" star, is not only a Texan but also—get this!—a singer.

Was it exciting to suddenly have a famous name?

"No! Annoying!" says the less-famous Clarkson.

The day after the younger Kelly Clarkson became the first *American Idol* winner, the older Kelly Clarkson called the phone company to demand an unlisted number. "They said, 'What's your name?' " she remembers. She told them. "There's a big intake of breath, and then, 'Oh, right away, Miss Clarkson! We understand entirely!' "

One time, though, the unfamous Clarkson had the tables turned for just a second. "I read an interview and someone asked [the *Idol* winner] how this new fame was affecting her, and she said it was strange: 'Someone has me married with, like, five kids or something.' And I thought, *That's me!*"

THE HIDDEN BOND

The weirdest thing about sharing a famous person's name is that, even though the two of you have nothing else in common, an invisible bond is formed. Just ask Phil Michaelson, founder of a tech company called KartMe. His name isn't exactly the same as that of Phil Mickelson, the professional golfer of enormous talent who just couldn't win a major. Still, when Mickelson finally clinched the Masters in 2004, says Michaelson, "I was very excited to have that weight lifted off our collective back."

For Dave Mathews, a tech guru, the opposite happened. Everyone loved the rocker until his tour bus driver dumped 800 pounds of bathroom waste on a steel-grid bridge in Chicago—with a tour boat cruising underneath. Suddenly, everyone was flooding the tech guy's blog with bile. He tried to correct folks: I'm a different Mathews! I invent things. I explain tech on TV. My last name has one *t*!

Didn't matter and still doesn't. He still gets the rock star's emails, blog hits and, when they once stayed at the same hotel, flowers. The card, from a nurse, gushed, "I can't tell you how much you mean to me."

Wow, thought our Dave: *She must really love my tech blog.*

Kansas City electronics engineering student Oprah Brown—named for some daytime TV talk show host—uses the connection to start conversations with strangers. "I'll call someone and say, 'This is Oprah.' They scream and get all excited." Then she adds that her last name is Brown. And that she's a collections agent. It goes downhill from there.

As for Charles "Buddy" Manson, it all went downhill in late 1969—when the police finally traced the murder of pregnant actress Sharon Tate and six others to the cult leader who shares his name. One of the 150 roughnecks Buddy was then supervising at a chemical company tacked the front-page story to a bulletin board.

For a while, Buddy considered changing his name. He railed at his father for giving it to him. But this Manson realized, a name is what you make of it. Now, when he checks into a hotel and the clerk looks a little leery, he leans in and whispers, "I just got out of jail."

I doubt they kick him out of a suite.

The author of *The Prince* thought it better to be feared than loved, instructing children to be cunning and cutthroat. Here's how Mr. Machiavelli would review more recent children's titles:

- ***Where the Wild Things Are*:** Max could have been a great and terrible ruler. But he let loneliness creep into his heart and gave up his position of power. I give this opus 3 out of 5 stars.
- ***Guess How Much I Love You*:** Love should be used only for deceitful means, and Little Nutbrown Hare understands that his father's love can be used to manipulate his actions. 4 stars.
- ***Charlotte's Web*:** Charlotte should have drained that pig for all he was worth. Instead, she made the mistake of having empathy for the weak hog. Pathetic. 1 weak dying star.
- ***The Very Hungry Caterpillar*:** The ambitious young caterpillar eats his way through bigger and more difficult obstacles and emerges more powerful than ever. 5 glorious stars.
- ***The Giving Tree*:** The boy uses fraud to deceive the tree into giving him more and more of itself. The ends always justify the means. 5 stars.

—POINTSINCASE.COM

My favorite novel is *The Hunchback of Notre Dame*. I just love a protagonist with a twisted back story.

—BESTLIFEONLINE.COM

"No one's winning. It's ballet."

I had a chance encounter with a pastor who told me about a wonderful event held at his church. "We had a singing group the other day that performed without instruments," he said.

"A cappella?" I asked.

He shrugged. "I don't remember the name of the group."

—WADE HAMPTON

I had just purchased a painting of the Last Supper when my young grandson came home. He studied it for a few minutes, then asked, "What are they doing, playing poker?"

—THERESA GALLEGOS

After reading a poem I'd labored over, my mother said, "This is good. Really good!"

I was beaming!

Then she felt compelled to ask, "Are you sure you wrote it?"

—THERESA BAUMBACH

Gilbert Gottfried on how he got into comedy: "I think I was too stupid to do anything else, and that stupidity helped me. Not only was I too stupid to do anything else, but I was too stupid to think of the odds against it."

—*EL PASO TIMES*

It's a truism: Ukulele players garner little respect. Once, at a bluegrass festival, I was invited onstage to jam with the band. The lead guitarist took one look at my uke and said, "You know you're not supposed to wash your guitar in hot water, don't you?"

—JOHN KLAPPROTH

My old music instructor told me that when she taught music in elementary schools, she began each session by having the class sing a familiar song. She said that one enthusiastic first grader stood out for his rendition of "God Bless America" when he belted out those stirring lyrics: "Stand beside her and guide her, through the night with a light from a bulb!"

—PAUL LUND

Replace one letter and suddenly these films don't seem quite so fearsome:

- *Apocalypse Cow*
- *Bill Bill*
- *HoboCop*
- *Mortal Wombat*
- *Top Nun*
- *The Silence of the Lamp*s
- *The Whining*

—BOREDPANDA.COM

Scene: An office

Employee #1: I want to start reading more books.

Employee #2: Didn't you just read yesterday?

—OVERHEARDINTHE OFFICE.COM

When electric keyboard player Johnny Greenwood joined the rock group Radiohead, he knew lead singer Thom Yorke had fired a previous keyboardist for playing too loudly. He came up with a novel way to stay employed: He turned off his instrument. During months of rehearsals, he says, "I'd pretend to play ... and Thom would say, 'I can't quite hear what you're doing, but I think you're adding a really interesting texture.'"

—NPR

Lately I go to the restroom at the movies but forget where I'm seated, then I return and just begin a new life in a new seat with a new family.

—@CONTWIXT

Among my all-time favorite movies is *Babe*. For years, whenever I wanted to compliment someone, I'd quote the film's famous line: "That'll do, Pig, that'll do."

Recently, I got my husband to watch the movie with me. When that scene came on, he turned to me, stunned.

"It's a compliment? All these years I thought you were insulting me!"

—TIGER MILLER

Future Stars

I showed my third grade music class a short film about composer George Frideric Handel. Afterward, a student asked if that was really Handel or an actor playing Handel.

"Well, Alex," I said, "Handel lived way back in the 1700s. Does that give you a hint?"

"Ah," said Alex, realizing his mistake. "It couldn't have been him. If it were really Handel from that long ago, the film would have been in black-and-white."

—PAULA FARINA

No offense to the von Trapps, but if I go to a lavish party and seven kids just start singing about how they have to go to bed, I'm using that time to refill my drink.

—@1FOLLOWERNODAD

You may be tough, but you're not "just sat through a fourth grade recorder concert" tough.

—@MCDADSTUFF

The girl I babysit has made me watch *Wall-E* at least 10 times, so I assumed it was her favorite movie. Today, her mom told me that she watches it because she thinks it's mine.

— @MADDIEPOOLEE

"And those are some of the books I would have read if the internet had never been invented."

"Do you have any true-crime podcasts?"

As a wannabe musician, I took advantage of an opportunity to play with a local recorder group. During a break in our first rehearsal, the woman next to me, an accomplished musician, said, "You have a beautiful vibrato!" I basked in the glow of her praise until she added, "You're not supposed to."

—VICKI MORRISON GOBLE

If rock bands ran the country, here are the departments they would run:

- **Joint Chiefs of Staff:** Motley Crue
- **Mission to the United Nations:** Foreigner
- **Environmental Protection Agency:** Green Day
- **Nuclear Regulatory Commission:** Canned Heat
- **U.S. Patent Office:** The Mothers of Invention
- **Amtrak:** Grand Funk Railroad
- **Federal Aviation Administration:** The B-52s
- **National Transportation Safety Board:** Crash Test Dummies

—ROGER DEAS 5577

After I sang a solo in church, an elderly gentleman offered me his highest compliment.

"I liked your song for two reasons," he said. "You sang it well, and you didn't sing too long."

—ANN ABERNATHY

Jurassic Park is a movie about how just because something is great it doesn't mean you should bring it back—and it has three sequels.

—@MEAKOOPA

I just want to be as happy as a character in the first half-hour of a horror movie.

—@MEGANAMRAM

Period shows from the Middle Ages and the Renaissance are big on Netflix, HBO and Amazon—*Medici* and *The Last Kingdom*, to name a couple. Here are a few of the more obscure characters you'll find way down on the credits:

- **The knight who was afraid to fight:** Sir Render
- **The undercover knight:** Sir Veillance
- **The knight who always guessed right:** Sir Miser
- **The knight who showed up unexpectedly:** Sir Prise
- **The knight who drank too much:** Sir Rhosis
- **The dancing knight:** Sir Prance-a-Lot
- **The loudest knight of them all:** Sir Roundsound
- **The foulmouthed knight:** Sir Cuss

—KINGDOMPURSUITS.COM

QUOTABLE QUOTES

THE LENGTH OF A FILM SHOULD BE DIRECTLY RELATED TO THE ENDURANCE OF THE HUMAN BLADDER.

—ALFRED HITCHCOCK

The play was a great success, but the audience was a disaster.

—OSCAR WILDE

I think my music is like anchovies—some people like it, some people get nauseous.

—BARRY MANILOW

My son does not appreciate classical musicians such as the Stones; he is more into bands with names like Heave and Squatting Turnips.

—DAVE BARRY

A bookstore is one of the only pieces of evidence we have that people are still thinking.

—JERRY SEINFELD

If you play a tune and a person don't tap their feet, don't play the tune.

—COUNT BASIE

Painting: The art of protecting flat surfaces from the weather and exposing them to the critic.

—AMBROSE BIERCE

The remarkable thing about Shakespeare is that he really is very good, in spite of all the people who say he is very good.

—ROBERT GRAVES

Too many pieces of music finish too long after the end.

—IGOR STRAVINSKY

Talking about music is like dancing about architecture.

—STEVE MARTIN

ANYBODY CAN DIRECT, BUT THERE ARE ONLY 11 GOOD WRITERS.

—MEL BROOKS

A VIRTUOSO AND ME

The great pianist displays a talent for acting

By Anne Semmes

itting at the piano, I'm about to play one of the few simple pieces I've mastered—barely a cut above "Twinkle, Twinkle Little Star." I have my best blue dress on and ribbons in my hair. Sprawled on the rug are our cocker spaniels, Rusty and Dusty.

During cocktail hour in 1950s St. Francisville, Louisiana, several Baton Rouge Symphony Orchestra musicians and guests of the board mingle in our living room. Daddy, highball in hand, smiles with pride.

"You can do it, Annie," he says, with his usual fatherly deaf ear to my flaws. His favorite music was Broadway show tunes, especially *South Pacific*. (When I hear snippets, I think of him.)

Nearby is my mother, who has more highfalutin musical taste. She'd taken my Brownie troop to see the orchestra, a first for the majority of my country classmates. One girl from rural Hardwood saw cellos and squealed, "Look at them big guitars, y'all!"

Back at our piano, I'm cornered. Standing close to me is an elegant Spanish woman in a silk dress, her raven hair in a bun. On her face is what can only be called a forced smile. She is world-renowned classical pianist Amparo Iturbi, best known for duets with her brother José. A few years before, the Iturbis had performed Mozart's Concerto for Two Pianos and Orchestra in E-Flat in New York City before a crowd of 12,000.

Now, as the orchestra's visiting performer, Amparo Iturbi is our guest, compelled to listen to ... me. A prodigy I am not. As I rush through the piece—more *presto* than stately *lento*—even the dogs shamble out of the room.

Fortunately, my recital is brief. She claps politely and says, "Brava!"

We have both put on a worthy performance.

WHAT'S UP,
DOC?

At the doctor's office, I saw a 20-something man trying to make an appointment for a Mrs. Brown. Try as he might, he just could not remember her first name. Frustrated, he left. A few minutes later, I passed him outside the office on the phone.

"Hey, Dad," he said. "What's Mom's first name?"

—JAMES SECOR

My aunt was in the hospital for hip-replacement surgery and not happy about having to wear the hospital garb she'd been given. So after she was wheeled into surgery, my mother ran out and bought her a nice robe to wear instead. Rather than being thankful, my aunt was appalled.

"You left the hospital while I was in surgery?" she asked. "What would you have done if I had died?"

"Well, first of all, I'd have returned the robe," answered Mom.

—SUE TIMMONS

After my wife accidentally swallowed my prostate medication, our daughter called a pharmacist to ask whether there was any cause for alarm. He replied, "Only if she starts hanging out at hardware stores and buys a lot of power tools."

—GARY MASSEY

I'm an EMT. I once responded to a man complaining of an insect crawling into his right ear. But more bothersome was the burning sensation in his left ear. That's when we noticed his wife holding a bottle of insect spray. Turns out, she had sprayed insecticide into his left ear thinking it would "flush" the insect out of his right ear. I had to explain to her that our ear canals are separated by our brain.

—REDDIT.COM

As my husband read his post-op instructions, one directive stood out: "You must sleep without pillows for 48 hours."

He was appalled, protesting, "I'm not sleeping that long!"

—NELLIE STROWBRIDGE

I told the kids I never want to live in a vegetative state, dependent on some machine and fluids from a bottle. So they unplugged my computer and threw out my wine.

—BEVERLY MCLAUGHLIN

Scene with a patient in my medical exam room:

Me: How old are your children?

Patient: They're 44 and 39 from my wife who passed away, and from my second wife, 15 and 13.

Me: That's quite the age difference!

Patient: Well, the older ones didn't give me any grandkids, so I made my own.

—MARIA MURILLO

Doctors and nurses in hospitals work long, strenuous hours. Sometimes it shows up in the odd things they accidentally write in the patient charts:

- "The patient is tearful and crying constantly. She also appears to be depressed."
- "On the second day the knee was better, and on the third day it had completely disappeared."
- "Bleeding began in the rectal area and continued all the way to Los Angeles."
- "She is numb from her toes down."
- "The skin was moist and dry."
- "Social history reveals this 1-year-old patient does not smoke or drink and is presently unemployed."
- "Patient has two teenage children but no other abnormalities."

—NURSEBUFF.COM AND NURSESLABS.COM

My mother has a medical podcast where she self-diagnoses her ailments. It's called my voicemail and it happens every morning at 9 a.m.

—@KIMMYMONTE

A serious lung problem landed me in a rehab center, connected to oxygen 24 hours a day. One day the oxygen ran low, so I asked an attendant for a fresh tank.

"You'll have to wait," she told me. "We're out of tanks and waiting for a delivery."

As she walked away, she muttered, "This wouldn't happen if patients would just stop using 'em all up."

—PHILLIP RADCLIFFE

Before my friend's dreaded hemorrhoid exam, the nurse tried to put her at ease by talking up her doctor's years of experience. Then she paused thoughtfully.

"The funny thing is," she said, "although he's an excellent proctologist, he started out wanting to be a dentist. But he couldn't stand bad breath."

—LUCRETIA MCCURLEY

Kudos to therapists for resisting the natural urge to top other people's problems.

—@JOSHCOMERS

MAD SCIENCE

The craziest discoveries, inventions and experiments ever!

By Andy Simmons

Innovation. It's what got us through the Dark Ages, polio and Celine Dion. And throughout history, prizes and accolades have been heaped on great scientific figures like Curie and Einstein who have helped move our society forward in leaps and bounds. But for every person who solves a great cosmic mystery or develops a miracle cure, there are thousands more who aimed much, much lower. Take, for example, Katherine K. Whitcome, the University of Cincinnati assistant professor who, along with her colleagues, published a paper explaining why pregnant women don't tip over. Groundbreaking stuff, right? Well, rest easy, because she, too, is a laureate—an Ig Nobel laureate. These tongue-in-cheek annual awards are bestowed upon those who dabble in some very strange science. Here are just a few past winners and their (Ig) noble endeavors.

PEACE PRIZE

Awarded to Stephan Bolliger, Steffen Ross, Lars Oesterhelweg, Michael Thali and Beat Kneubuehl of the University of Bern, Switzerland, for determining which hurts more—being smashed over the head with a full beer bottle or an empty one.

An inherent problem in an experiment of this nature is finding volunteers who will agree to be brained with a bottle in the name of science. The scientists overcame this obstacle by dropping steel balls onto full and empty beer bottles. They found that the empties were sturdier than their full brethren because the gas pressure from the liquid produces additional strain on the glass. Needless to say, full or not, beer bottles can cause a whole lot of hurt, which is why the scientists advocate prohibiting them "in situations [that] involve risk of human conflicts." Of course, if we outlaw beer bottles, only outlaws will drink beer from bottles.

MEDICINE PRIZE

Awarded to Donald L. Unger of Thousand Oaks, California, for investigating a possible cause of arthritis of the fingers, by cracking the knuckles of his left hand—but never the knuckles of his right hand—twice a day for 60 years.

After being warned by his mother to swear off that demon knuckle cracking, young Donald Unger tested the accuracy of this hypothesis on himself. More than 219,000 cracked knuckles later, the verdict is in: Crack away. Unger could detect no difference between the two hands, and he found no evidence of arthritis. From why you shouldn't run with scissors to why you should wait an hour after eating before you swim, Unger's seminal research has thrown everything our mothers told us into question.

VETERINARY MEDICINE PRIZE

Awarded to Catherine Douglas and Peter Rowlinson of Newcastle University, United Kingdom, for showing that cows that have names give more milk than nameless cows.

Admit it, when was the last time you paid a compliment to a heifer? Or told one, "You're a thousand roast beef sandwiches wrapped in a gorgeous leather jacket"? It turns out our attitudes make a difference. Being friendly and remembering a cow's name can increase milk yield by 258 liters a year. This came as no surprise to farmers, one of whom told the researchers that cows "hurt and love like anyone else."

CHEMISTRY PRIZE

Awarded to Javier Morales, Miguel Apátiga and Victor M. Castaño of Universidad Nacional Autónoma de México, for creating diamonds from tequila.

As if there weren't already enough reasons to love tequila! It seems we can spill a little on the bar and make diamonds. Of course, you have to heat it up to 536 degrees and do a bunch of other stuff to it before you can place it on your main squeeze's finger. But the first round is on us!

BIOLOGY PRIZE

Awarded to Fumiaki Taguchi, Song Guofu and Zhang Guanglei of Kitasato University Graduate School of Medical Sciences in Japan, for demonstrating that kitchen refuse can be reduced by more than 90 percent by using an enzyme-producing bacteria extracted from the feces of giant pandas.

While this could have valuable applications—reducing garbage and waste—it still raises the question: How did it dawn on someone to try this experiment? And, of course, if one of your aims in ridding yourself of garbage is to get rid of the stench, adding poop to it is not likely to help.

"You're more than just a patient to me, Mrs. Melnik. You're a potential medical journal article."

My husband is a physician and uses a dictation service to transcribe his oral notes. On occasion the typists have accidentally altered the sentence structure or words, resulting in something my husband had not necessarily intended. For example, one transcriber wrote, "The patient is recently married; otherwise, he is normal and healthy."

—ELAINE EHRENPREIS

I was an hour late for my appointment at the sleep disorder clinic. My excuse: "I overslept."

—LOU FLEURY

A patient walks into his doctor's office and hands him a note that says, "I can't talk! Help me!"

"OK," says the doctor. "Put your thumb on the table." The man doesn't understand why that would help, but he does what he's told. The doctor picks up a huge book and drops it on the man's thumb.

"AAAAAAAA!" the man yells.

"Good," says the doctor. "Come back tomorrow and we'll work on *B*."

—VALOURDIGEST.COM

A friend took her son to the doctor's office after he sprained his finger. The nurse applied a splint, only to be told she'd put it on the wrong finger.

"I'm sorry," she said.

"That's OK," my friend's son said. "You were only off by one digit."

—PRUDENCE PERRY

As a brain wave technologist, I often ask postoperative patients to smile to make sure their facial nerves are intact. It always struck me as odd to be asking this question right after brain surgery, so a colleague suggested I ask patients to show me their teeth. Armed with this new phrase, I said to my next patient, "Mr. Smith, show me your teeth."

He shook his head.

"The nurse has them."

—EMILY MURPHY

While celebrating an auspicious milestone, our university medical school ordered 2,000 pens with the inscription "Faculty of Medicine" to hand out to guests. When the pens arrived, all 2,000 had this inauspicious message: "Faulty of Medicine."

—ROBERT HALSTEAD

I advised a patient to fast for 12 hours before his upcoming medical procedure. With a look of great concern, he asked, "All at once?"

—RUTH LEE

Three weeks after my total knee replacement, I had my first outpatient visit with the surgeon. When the office visit was over, my wife left ahead of me to get the car. I walked with my cane through the lobby. As I approached the exit and started to press the automatic door button, I noticed an elderly gentleman approaching from the other side. To be courteous, I waited for him to enter first. Only then did I realize I was looking at my own reflection in the door.

—GREGORY LARKIN

Unless she is "near death," as she puts it, my mom refuses to go to the doctor. Recently, she noticed her doctor at a church reception. The man nodded and smiled at her, and she walked over to join him at the dessert table.

"I really need to call you for a visit," she confided. "I know it's been a while." He nodded knowingly, and she leaned closer to whisper into his ear, "You know, I would come see you more often if you wouldn't ask me to take off my clothes every time."

A red flush crept up the man's neck, and he shook his head and smiled.

"I believe you must have me confused with someone else," he said. "Perhaps your doctor?"

—JAN SEMPLE MCKINNEY

Ever since the coronavirus outbreak, my 47-year-old son has been washing his hands religiously. In fact, he said, "I've been washing my hands so much, I found the answers to an old eighth-grade math quiz."

—SUSAN FREEMAN

Nursing can be a dirty business, as I discovered while helping my grumpy patient change his colostomy bag. You can imagine the smell. Still, I soldiered on, telling myself to think about the patient's feelings and not let my queasiness show. That all changed when he turned to me, scrunched his nose and said, "God, you've got bad breath!"

—AN ANONYMOUS NURSE, ON BUSINESSINSIDER.COM

I'm supposed to give my wife an injection today but she's worried cuz she's seen my many struggles with Capri Sun straws.

—@DADDYGOFISH

While volunteering in a hospital during college, I was tasked with feeding an elderly patient who didn't have the strength to do it himself. When his tray arrived, I picked up the utensils and asked, "Would you like me to use a spoon or a fork?"

He replied, "That depends on your aim."

—SANDY SPEER

Baby Blues

I was very pregnant when my husband and I visited our ob-gyn for a routine appointment. When the doctor noticed that the baby's heart rate was slow, he decided that I should be induced. Or, as my husband, for whom English is a second language, explained to my mother, "The doctor wants to seduce her."

—SARAH B.

I received a call from a customer on our pharmacy benefits hotline saying that she could not get in touch with her doctor and thus couldn't get her birth control prescription filled. Although I explained there was nothing I could do, she became irate.

"Fine!" she said. "But if I get pregnant, it will be your fault!"

—DAVID FLOYD

I was in the emergency room when a young male nurse came in to ask routine medical questions.

Nurse: Have you ever had a hysterectomy?
Me: Yes.
Nurse: When?
Me: 2011.
Nurse: Do you think you could be pregnant?
Me: Do you think this is the right career for you?

—RACHELLE KARMAN

I work in a small community hospital and often draw blood samples from inpatients. One evening, while I was preparing to take blood from an elderly patient, she stated, "I can feel it in my bones." Perplexed, I replied, "But I haven't even stuck you yet." She said no and motioned to the television. She was solving a puzzle on *Wheel of Fortune*!

—MELINDA ANDRE-ECHOLS

One of my favorite games to play is "Is my headache from dehydration, caffeine withdrawal, lack of proper nutrition, my ponytail, stress, lack of sleep, not wearing my glasses, or brain tumor?"

—@PMILBS_

As a pharmacist, I often counsel patients on their new medications. One day, I was informing a woman about the side effects of her prescription, specifically drowsiness.

"You won't be able to work or drive while you're taking this," I told her. "Do you have any questions?"

Her little boy, who had been quietly standing next to her, raised his hand.

"Can she still cook?" he asked.

"Of course she can," I replied.

His mother explained ruefully, "He was hoping you'd say no."

—LITA HERNANDEZ

As we watched a program about a man with agoraphobia, my wife asked, "Is that a disability?"

"Yes," I answered.

"Maybe I have that."

I shook my head. "No. He's afraid to leave the house. You just like to stay home."

—JEFF PETERSON

This actual text exchange proves that some wrong numbers turn out right:

Matt: Hey Dr. Park, this is Matt from the vascular lab, I have a patient here with an external iliac occlusion with cold foot pain and numbness that started three days ago. What should I do with her?

Hannah: Hi, this is Hannah. I think you have the wrong number, but I Googled it and I'm pretty sure you need to put a stent in her left radial artery. Best of luck, Matt!

Matt: Sorry, wrong-number Hannah. She ended up actually getting a stent. Took about three hours longer for trained medical professionals to figure out what took you about five minutes, great job.

Hannah: Ya hiring?

—ELITEDAILY.COM

I'd never had surgery, and I was nervous.

"This is a very simple, non-invasive procedure," the anesthesiologist reassured me. I felt better, until ...

"Heck," he continued, "you have a better chance of dying from the anesthesia than the surgery itself."

—T.F.

My uncle was in the hospital when a nurse came into his room and asked him, "Do you use oxygen?" With an incredulous look on his face, my uncle replied, "Doesn't everybody?"

—ROBERT WILLIAMSON

"It could be nothing, or it could be the beginning of an omelet."

James received a bill for his recent surgery and was astonished to see a $900 charge for the anesthesiologist. He called the office to demand an explanation.

"Is this some kind of mistake?" he asked when he got the doctor on the phone.

"No, not at all," the doctor said calmly.

"Well," said James, irritated, "that's awfully costly for just knocking someone out!"

"Not really," replied the doctor. "I knocked you out for free. The $900 is for bringing you back."

—ARKY MUSCATO

There are more than 68,000 medical billing codes that doctors use to denote injuries and maladies for insurance purposes. These actual codes are among the more specific ones:

- **W59.22XA:** Struck by turtle
- **Y93.D1:** Stabbed while crocheting
- **Z63.1:** Problems in relationship with in-laws
- **V91.07XD:** Burn due to water skis on fire
- **V97.33XD:** Sucked into jet engine

—HEALTHCAREDIVE.COM AND ADVANCED DATA SYSTEMS CORPORATION

It was my first night caring for an elderly patient. When he grew sleepy, I wheeled his chair as close to the bed as possible and, using the techniques I'd learned in nursing school, grasped him in a bear hug to lift him onto the bed. But I couldn't clear the top of the mattress. So I grabbed him again, summoned all my might and hoisted him successfully onto the bed. When the night shift nurse arrived a few hours later, I recounted what had happened.

"Funny," she said, looking puzzled. "Usually I just ask him to get in bed, and he does."

—ERIN DOCKERY

Quick Quips

Who called it your foot falling asleep and not coma toes?

—@CHUUEW

In England, "booster shot" is spelled "borchestershire shot."

—@SARAHSURGEY1

If you're thinking what I'm thinking, here's my therapist's number.

—@TOPAZ_KELL

The doctor gave me some cream for my skin rash. He said I was a sight for psoriasis.

—BESTLIFEONLINE.NET

To the guy who stole my antidepressants, I hope you're happy now.

—@EDDYELFENBEIN

I called the tinnitus hotline, but it just kept ringing ...

—E.M.

A nervous patient arrived at our dental office for root canal surgery. He was brought into the examination room and then left alone for a few minutes. When the dentist returned, he found the patient standing next to a tray of surgical equipment, rifling through the tools.

"What are you doing?" the dentist asked.

The patient replied, "Removing the ones I don't like."

—GCFL.NET

E
I E
I O E
I E I O E
I E I O E I E
Reynolds

"It's serious. There are no TED Talks for what you have."

WORRIED SICK

That little mole, persistent cough or nasty itch must be a sign of a rare and fatal disease, right? Our resident M.D. and his assistant are here to soothe your fevered brow.

By Billy Goldberg, M.D., and Mark Leyner

There's a venerable Chinese proverb that says "Give a man a fish and you feed him for a day. Teach a man to fish and you feed him for a lifetime." The hypochondriac's version is "Give a man a symptom and he'll worry for a day. Give him access to Google and he'll torture himself for a lifetime." If you've been spending a little too much time online—and way too much time in abject terror—I'm here to help, with assistance from my literary (and medically savvy) scrub nurse, Mark Leyner. I've been an ER doctor for almost 20 years, and I've treated everything from leprosy to lumbago. I've seen innocent freckles that turned out to be deadly skin cancers and many more that were just innocent freckles. My job is to find out which camp you're in. Got an itch, rash, cough or funny sound that keeps you up at night? Tell me all about it.

DEAR DR. BILLY,

I hear this weird popping sound when I move my right wrist in a certain way. Sometimes I feel it too. I'm 16, so it's not early arthritis or some other serious condition ... is it?

Don't worry—you're not turning into bubble wrap. It's perfectly normal for your joints to make a popping sound. The noise is produced when little bubbles burst in the lubricating fluid surrounding the joint. Some people even get a kick out of making this sound by cracking their knuckles, which, by the way, won't lead to arthritis, despite the admonitions of many parents. Wrist popping, although it has never achieved the widespread popularity of knuckle cracking, is likely equally innocuous. Look at it this way: Next time you're in your flamenco class, you'll be the one who doesn't need castanets.

DEAR DR. BILLY,

I spent a happy Sunday afternoon in my garden pruning my rosebushes and mulching my flower beds. That night, I began to experience a weird itching on my hand. I also felt extremely fatigued, with back pain and aching calf muscles. I called my brother-in-law (an insomniac amateur infectious disease specialist and general know-it-all). I could hear him typing away on his laptop, and within a minute or two, he grimly announced, "You've got sporotrichosis. You'd better get your affairs in order."

Tell your brother-in-law to get his own affairs in order. It's most likely that your hand itches because it's dry; maybe you also exposed it to something that you're slightly allergic to or that irritated your skin. You're fatigued because you worked all day in your garden. Your muscles ache because you're not used to being hunched over a hoe for 12 hours. Even if your hand is red and swollen and oozing pus and you have a fever, there's a good possibility you have a simple infection that an antibiotic will easily cure. Call your brother-in-law back—preferably right after he falls asleep—and inform him that sporotrichosis, an infection caused by a fungus that grows on plants, occurs in just one or two people per million in the United States. And even in the unlikely event that you're the one in a million, the infection is easily treated with an antifungal medication. I recommend gardening gloves and a moratorium on late-night calls to Dr. Doom.

"I recommend gardening gloves and a moratorium on late-night calls to Dr. Doom."

DEAR DR. BILLY,

For the past two months, I've been having headaches in the front of my head—basically in my temples, sometimes right, sometimes left. I've tried aspirin, Tylenol, Advil, cold compresses. Nothing works. So now I'm convinced I have terminal brain cancer. I've started working on my

will when the pain lets up (which makes my new boyfriend irate because I haven't left him my red Miata convertible). I spend most of my free time reading about gliomas and blastomas online and watching movies on Netflix about people with brain tumors. Help!

You like movies? Skip *Dark Victory*, and rent *Kindergarten Cop*. Then imagine the Teutonic tones of the movie's Detective John Kimble, aka the ex-governor of California, telling you, "It's not a tumor!" There are innumerable possible reasons for your headaches, but least likely among them is a brain tumor. A better bet: You're suffering from stress, tension, allergies, sinus infections or teeth grinding. Or you might just need a new prescription for your glasses or contact lenses.

In the ER, there are a few questions we ask when someone comes in with a headache: Was it a sudden onset of the worst headache of your life? (Makes us think of a ruptured aneurysm.) Do you have a fever and a stiff neck? (Makes us think of meningitis.) Is your headache consistent but worse in the morning and accompanied by vomiting, seizures, visual changes, or weakness in your limbs? (Makes us think it could be a brain tumor—but even then, the odds are against it.)

If you have any of those more serious warning signs, see your doctor, who may suggest that you consult a neurologist. In any case, try to relax, since stress about your headache is probably adding to it. And ditch the guy who seems to covet your Miata more than he covets you.

DEAR DR. BILLY,

Lately my ear canals have been very itchy. There's also a slight discharge that is clear and watery and sometimes a little sticky. I have come to the conclusion that it's a food allergy, but I haven't been able to pinpoint which food.

The reason you haven't been able to identify the offending food is that this is most likely not a food allergy. Although you wouldn't know it from the enormous amount of airtime health-oriented talk shows devote to the subject, serious food allergies are not very common. According to a report published in the *Journal of the American Medical Association*, while nearly 3 out of 10 people think they have food allergies, less than 5% of adults and 8% of kids actually do. In fact, researchers who examined more than 12,000 studies found that when the right test was used, even people who had gotten a doctor's diagnosis had a less than 50-50 chance of being truly allergic.

If your waxy buildup isn't from a food allergy, what's the problem? I'd put my money on an outer ear infection, or, to be fancy, otitis externa. That's an inflammation or infection of the external auditory canal—the tube that runs from the outer ear to the middle ear. The condition is also known as swimmer's ear because it's most common in people who are regularly submerged in water. It can be addressed by a visit to your doctor and some antibiotic drops.

The other possibility is that you just have some excess earwax. But don't go reaching for a Q-tip! The ear is self-cleaning and usually produces the right amount of wax necessary for its own protection. Cotton-tipped swabs tend to pack the wax in and can cause pain or even a perforated eardrum. If your ears are impacted with wax—you'll know it if you can barely hear—you need to break up the plug. You can try this at home with over-the-counter products, but if a solid nugget has formed, you are going to need a pro to do the excavating.

DEAR DR. BILLY,

Since we moved to Florida in 2002, my mom, my sister and I have developed bumps on our backs. (I checked online, and they look like lipomas.) My friend, who lives nearby, also has one on her back. And a friend of hers, who has one too, consulted her doctor, who said they come from all the hormones added to the chicken we eat.

Although it's difficult to diagnose anything without seeing it, you may be absolutely correct in the first part of your diagnosis. Lipomas are benign tumors composed of mature fat cells. They tend to be painless and soft to the touch, and they move a little when you press on them. They're the most common noncancerous tumor in all adults, striking 1% of the population. They are seen mostly in women (and are known to run in families), so it's not surprising that you, your mom and your friends share this lumpy affliction.

Usually you don't need to do anything about lipomas unless they become bothersome. Then the treatment is simple surgical removal.

Now for your chicken theory. There are many concerns about how environmental hormones might be affecting our health, but hormones are not used in chicken production. So you and your family can keep this item on the menu. That said, I'd probably stay away from the KFC Original Recipe Double Down Sandwich. It won't give you a new lipoma, but it might pack on the pounds.

DEAR DR. BILLY,

Recently I started to notice a tingling in my left hand. It's worse when I wake up in the morning, but it's been three days, and it's still there. I looked it up online, and now I'm sure I have a benign spinal tumor or lumbar spinal stenosis, or maybe I've had a stroke. The Mayo Clinic website says tingling in parts of the body is a

sign of multiple sclerosis. What do I do next? There are 930,000 more Google hits for "tingling fingers," and I don't think I have that much time left.

If you don't have a family history of the disease, the odds of your having MS are really quite small. Ditto for things like spinal tumors and stenosis. Do you sleep with your hand under the pillow? Squashing it that way could be disrupting blood flow. Do you perform any repetitive movements, like typing on a keyboard and looking up disease symptoms all day? Carpal tunnel syndrome is a much more likely culprit in that case. Is your wristwatch too tight? Even that could cause needles and pins. Relax. MS is one of the hypochondriac's worst enemies. Its symptoms can be vague and tend to be things we all experience from time to time. If the tingling persists for more than a week, or if it's accompanied by double vision, a tremor or weakness in the limbs, or if the symptoms get worse when your body temperature goes up—say, when you take a hot bath—your doctor may want you to see a neurologist. But you're probably fine.

DEAR DR. BILLY,

I'm embarrassed to even write about this because it's a little gross. I keep coughing up these stinky little white things. They look like corn kernels but smell like toe jam. Help! What are these white smelly clumps in the back of my throat?

Your malodorous mouth balls are called tonsilloliths, or tonsil stones. These hard lumps are formed in the nooks and crannies of the tonsils and contain food particles, calcium and magnesium salts, bacteria, and sometimes small amounts of keratin. The bacteria produce volatile sulfur compounds (such as methyl mercaptan and dimethyl sulfide) that can make your breath smell bad. It's not known how common tonsil stones are, because most people swallow them without ever noticing. Brush your teeth, gargle and avoid eating right before bed, and you'll be less likely to get them.

So my advice to you is twofold: Stop worrying about those gross little balls, and never feel ashamed about talking to someone (especially your doctor) about your health. We're all human, and we produce an astonishing variety of smelly, disgusting and mysterious secretions.

Here's another rule of thumb: If you're experiencing new symptoms, sure, go online and do a little amateur medical sleuthing. But don't let all that information whip you into a frenzy of unbridled anxiety. If you're worried, see your doctor and have a frank, open conversation. That's the most efficient way to calm yourself down and treat what ails you—even if it's all in your head.

"Mr. Syms came out of the surgery OK, but he's on his way back to the recovery room after seeing the bill."

The irate daughter of one of our nursing home residents stormed into my office demanding answers. She had just read her father's chart and couldn't understand why he was so disliked by the staff. It took a while, but I was finally able to explain to her that the offending comment on the chart, "SOB," was a nursing abbreviation for "short of breath."

—DENNIS BECHMANN

Four Emergency Room nurses share their strangest stories on Reddit:

- I asked a patient complaining of dizziness if she'd ever been diagnosed with vertigo. Her daughter shook her head.

  "No, no," she said. "Mom's a Libra."

  —TBMTONADA

- It was 3 a.m. when a well-dressed man came in with his 8-year-old, healthy-looking son.

  "What's the problem?" I asked.

  He replied, "Well, I was at a wedding and it occurred to me that my son is a little short. Can you give him something to make him taller?"

  —SXHPOTT1

- I once had a patient tell me he needed his "decapitation medicine." It took a minute before I realized he was asking for his constipation medication.

  —NURSEMORBID

- A man once came in with a minor eye puncture. He had wanted to see what it looked like to have a bow and arrow aimed at him, so he aimed a drawn arrow at his reflection in a mirror and accidentally fired it. The arrow bounced off the mirror and proceeded to hit him in the eye.

  —TAPIRSAURUSREX

—NURSEBUFF.COM

Two psychiatrists pass each other in a hallway. One says, "Hey, how are you doing?" The other thinks to himself, I wonder what he meant by that ...

—SOUMYA PANDALAI

"Health-care workers are so stressed these days," I observed as my nurse in the hospital shut off an annoying and pointless machine alarm.

"The beeping all the time from these things doesn't help," she agreed. "Especially when you read that."

She pointed to the monitor instructions: "Press OK, then run."

—CAROLYN FRITSCHLE

Decided that the one phrase I do not want in my obituary is "died before his Botox doctor could revive him."

—@CONANOBRIEN

QUOTABLE QUOTES

NEVER, UNDER ANY CIRCUMSTANCES, TAKE A SLEEPING PILL AND A LAXATIVE AT THE SAME TIME.

—DAVE BARRY

Health nuts are going to feel stupid someday, lying in hospitals dying of nothing.

—REDD FOXX

I wonder why you can always read a doctor's bill and you can never read his prescription.

—FINLEY PETER DUNNE

I did some research, and it turns out I'm super Irish. Even my blood type is O apostrophe.

—BRIAN KILEY

I went to the doctor and he said, "You've got hypochondria." I said, "Not that as well!"

—TIM VINE

The only way to keep your health is to eat what you don't want, drink what you don't like and do what you'd rather not.

—MARK TWAIN

My doctor told me to stop having intimate dinners for four. Unless there are three other people.

—ORSON WELLES

The first wealth is health.

—RALPH WALDO EMERSON

Never go to a doctor whose office plants have died.

—ERMA BOMBECK

First the doctor gave me the good news: I was going to have a disease named after me.

—STEVE MARTIN

EAT RIGHT, EXERCISE REGULARLY, DIE ANYWAY.

—UNKNOWN

IN STITCHES

When it comes to mask-making, one Singer sewing machine has a lot to say

By Mariah Julio

n imagined dialogue between a woman and her sewing machine:

Singer: Well, well, well. You again. It's been a long while.

Me: I know. I've had a lot going on.

Singer: Uh-huh, sure.

Me: I'm here because I've got an urgent project to work on. People need masks right now.

Singer: You left me in your closet for a year, and now you want me to help you out, just like that?

Me: This could be your chance to shine again!

Singer: Do you even remember how to thread me?

Me: I can figure it out. Now, come on, we have work to do.

Singer: My bobbin is stuck. We're not doing anything.

Me: Look, it's a scary time. Let's work together. Your country needs you to make masks to help prevent a terrible disease.

Singer: You didn't mention being so patriotic when you bought me.

Me: It never came up.

Singer: A terrible disease, you say? Can I catch it?

Me: No, but you can help prevent it.

Singer: All right, maybe add a drop or two of oil to my bobbin case.

Me: I knew I could count on you. Does that feel better?

Singer: Much better. Let's go!

[A few days later]

Me: I think that's enough for now. Look at all these masks we've made!

Singer: Are you going to put me back in the closet?

Me: Yes. But don't be sad. I couldn't have done this without you.

Singer: Will you pat my case once in a while to let me know that I'm appreciated? That's all I really want.

Me: I understand. We all want that. I'm very proud of you.

[A few months later]

Me: Well, I just got a call. We need to sew more masks.

Singer: I knew you'd be back!

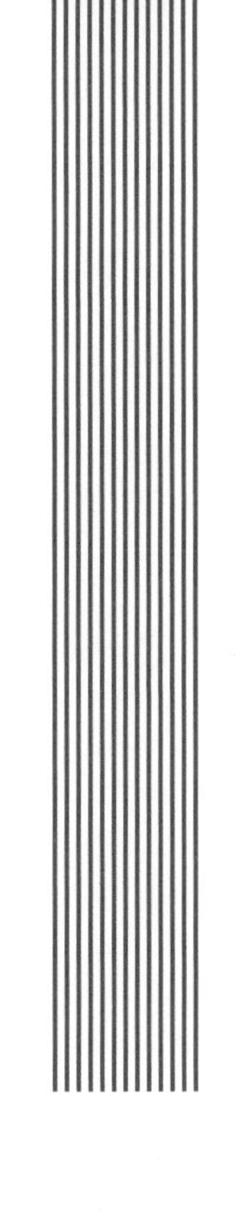

PLANES,
TRAINS
& AUTOMOBILES

While my wife may not be a car fanatic, she insists that the vehicle she drives fulfill certain criteria. One day she announced, "I know exactly what kind of car I want next."

"Oh, yeah?" I asked. "What kind?"

"Green."

—DALE DILDY

An airplane encounters turbulence and starts rocking from side to side. The flight crew quickly wheels out the drinks cart for the jittery passengers.

"Would you like a drink?" the flight attendant asks a businesswoman.

"Yes," she replies. "I'll have whatever the pilot's having."

—AJOKEADAY.COM

Car commercials grossly overestimate how much time I spend driving around in the desert.

—@TASTEFACTORY

An Uber is cruising down a boulevard when it runs a red light.

"Hey!" the passenger shouts. "Be careful!"

"Don't worry," says the driver. "My brother does it all the time."

He barrels through the next red light, and the passenger screams, "Stop doing that!"

"As I said, my brother does this all the time."

They approach the next light. Just when it turns green, the driver slams on the brakes. The confused passenger asks, "You just ran two red lights; why'd you stop at a green?"

"I had to," says the driver. "My brother might have been coming."

—DAVID MASELLA

As I struggled to start the gray Plymouth Voyager, I noticed a lady glaring at me through the driver's side window. I realized only then that I was in the wrong car. I got out of the minivan and apologized profusely, explaining that my vehicle was identical. I prayed that she didn't recognize me as the new school superintendent. As I walked away, I recalled that my wife had the Voyager. I had taken our green Volkswagen bug. The lady continued to stare at me as I got in and drove away.

—BOB FONTAINE

When I started learning how to drive, my dad, completely serious, said to me, "Always weave a little, and all the other cars will stay away from you."

—KARLEN STEPHENSEN

After we passed the same off-ramp for the third time, it was clear that I was lost. My little girl asked, "Daddy, do you know where you're going?"

"No," I said.

Her reply: "Then why are you still going there?"

—DAVE ARANDA-RICHARDS

A young man was trying to park his car between two others. He put it in reverse, and *bang*—he rammed right into the car behind him. He then went forward, and *bang*—he rammed right into the car in front. A young woman watching the maneuver couldn't contain herself.

"Do you always park by ear?" she asked.

—VENDERCI MARTINS VALENTE

Tanned, relaxed and unshaven, I landed at the Denver airport after coming back from my bucolic Caribbean vacation. As the customs agent handed my passport back to me, she cheerily welcomed me home by declaring, "Back to reality for you!"

—BRUCE NEAL

Quick Quips

I bought a pistachio-colored Mitsubishi, and I can't open it.

—@OFFBEATOLIV

St. Patrick drove all the snakes out of Ireland. They gave him a great Uber rating.

—@ROLLININTHESEAT

Not to brag, but I just filled up the gas tank and doubled the value of my car.

—@MOONSTRUCKINNYC

A journey of a thousand miles begins with running back in the house for something you forgot.

—@STEVEKOEHLER22

The tenth *Fast and Furious* movie should be called *Fast 10: Your Seat Belts.*

—@SOPHIEKEEN

The worst thing about parallel parking is witnesses.

—@ARMYVET1972

I'M A HERO BEHIND THE WHEEL

A rental car can make vacation travel easier—but only if you can actually get where you need to go

By Richard Glover

The automobile industry is spending billions of dollars on self-driving cars, just so we can sit in the backseat being chauffeured around. But what if we really like driving?

On vacation a few years ago, I spent hours being transported on trains, buses and planes. You sit there, bored and fidgeting. You read a novel for a while, then stare glumly out the window. You wonder if the bus driver or train driver or pilot could do with a little bit of assistance.

You've been turned into cargo, being shifted from one location to another.

Then, finally, comes the section of the vacation during which you hire a set of wheels. Oh boy. Suddenly, the cargo has been given agency.

After years of marriage, it's not often that you receive unalloyed praise from your partner, but on the highways of Crete, Greece, compliments come with every successful maneuver.

"Oh, well done!" says Jocasta, her voice full of admiration, as I navigate a roundabout without killing us both.

Better still, the rented car has gears, as opposed to my automatic-transmission vehicle back home. Into the roundabout I go, shifting down as we enter, then back up to fourth gear as we return to a straightaway. Really, it's like driving in a Formula One race.

We turn right, then right again, following the GPS navigation, and find ourselves in a small Cretan town. I speak sternly to the GPS: "We don't want to be here; we want the highway."

It instructs me to turn right once more. With every turn, the street narrows. It's like being in a magical shrinking room.

We retract the side mirrors. We take another turn. The new road is even narrower, the walls so close you feel compelled to hold your breath.

Another car appears, coming toward us from the opposite direction. The driver gesticulates, telling me I'll have to make way. But how? I don't have the nerve to back up along the impossibly narrow road.

Locals emerge. Soon there's a whole group—friendly, helpful—using sign language to suggest a solution.

There's a narrow garage opening to one side, a minuscule side street to the other. If I can squeeze the car forward into the garage, I could then, through a series of microscopic adjustments, back into the side street, allowing the other car to pass.

More locals arrive, standing on various sides of the vehicle, helpfully indicating that I have a centimeter to spare here, a millimeter there, and, really, I could afford to swing in harder on the right rear.

There are brick walls on all 17 sides of the car.

There's zero chance I won't damage the vehicle. This is significant since, a day earlier at the Europcar counter, I had refused the additional insurance, despite Jocasta's strenuous insistence that it was the sensible option.

I put it this way: "Everyone knows it's a rip-off. Besides, I don't intend to crash the car."

To which Jocasta responded: "That's the most stupid thing you've ever said, and, Lord, there's some competition."

Back in the small town, more locals continue to arrive. Soon it will be the mayor and a brass band.

One lady stands at the rear of the vehicle, waving me on. She's making vigorous "this way, this way" movements with her arms, which, translated from the Greek, mean "Oh, get on with it. There are at least 3 centimeters between you and this wall. What's so difficult?"

In an act of blind trust, I follow her instructions, creeping backward and forward. Remarkably, it works. I complete my 27-point turn into the side street, with no damage to the car.

The other vehicle passes. The driver gives me a grateful wave. I follow her lead, down the narrow lane and—finally—back onto the highway.

Free of the town, I pull over. My hands are trembling. I get out of the car, breathe in and out to steady my nerves, then reluctantly climb back behind the wheel.

Jocasta swivels toward me. "You're my hero," she says. I glance toward her, expecting the shadow of a teasing smile, but can find none.

"You're my hero," she repeats. She squeezes my hand.

We set off again. Before long, we head into another roundabout and emerge alive on the other side. "Well done," says Jocasta.

I accelerate. Third gear, fourth—I may choose to go into fifth.

Who'd swap this for a self-drive car?

"Of course, it's nothing serious, honey ... just a flooded engine."

My neighbor was working in his yard when suddenly a car came crashing through his hedge and ended up on his front lawn. He rushed to help the driver, an elderly lady.

"You appear a bit old to be driving," he said.

"I am!" she replied proudly. "I'm so old that I don't even need a license anymore."

"Really?" he asked skeptically. "And how did you manage that?"

"The last time I went to my doctor," she explained, "he asked to see my license. Then he said, 'You won't be needing this anymore,' cut it up and threw it away. So I thanked him and drove home!"

—PLANET PROCTOR NEWSLETTER

These may be some of the more creative justifications for speeding that police officers have encountered:

- *"I wasn't speeding; I just got a haircut and it makes me look fast."*
- *"I thought the sign I-95 meant the speed limit."*
- *"I have a cold, and when I cough, my foot mashes the pedal."*

—POLICEONE.COM

Sister Mary donned her habit and got into her vintage auto. About a mile down the road, she ran out of gas. Fortunately, there was a gas station on the next block, so she walked over. But when she got there, it was out of gas cans.

Sister Mary walked back to her car and opened the trunk to look for a container. All she could find was a bedpan. She walked back to the station and filled the bedpan as best she could. Then she walked back to her auto and began pouring gas from the bedpan into the tank.

From across the street, two Baptist ministers were watching all of this. One minister turned to the other and said, "If that car starts, I'm converting to Catholicism."

—JOHN MENDONCA

A man was driving on the highway when all of a sudden he had to swerve to avoid a box falling off the truck that was in front of him. Seconds later, a police officer pulled him over for reckless driving. As the officer was writing a ticket, the driver noticed that the box he'd avoided had been full of nails and tacks.

"I had to swerve or I'd have run over those and blown my tires!" he protested.

"OK," replied the officer, ripping up the ticket, "but I'm still bringing you in."

"What for?!"

"Tacks evasion."

—THEALTERNATIVE ACCOUNTANT.COM

A small plane with an instructor and a student on board hit the runway and bounced repeatedly until it came to a stop. The instructor turned to the student and said, "That was a very bad landing you just made."

"Me?" replied the student. "I thought *you* were landing!"

—*THE COCKLE BUR*

Helplessly lost in a small town in upstate New York, I waved down a passing police officer. Turns out the address I was looking for was in the opposite direction.

"Is it OK if I make a U-turn?" I asked.

"If I don't see you," he said, walking back to his car.

I quickly did a U-turn and got about a block before he came up behind me and pulled me over. Ambling over, he said, "I saw you."

—BARBARA HONIG

Based on a survey of yard signs in my neighborhood, it appears "Drive Like Your Kids Live Here" has a slight lead over both the Democratic and Republican candidates.

—@TUSOONSHAKUR

Every spring, my wife, Leah, and I make the three-day pilgrimage to Sanibel Island, Florida, from Grand Rapids, Michigan. My favorite parts of the drive are the farms, the blue sky and the trees coming into bloom. For Leah, it's the antique shops.

If we're within 100 yards of an antique shop, a flea market or a garage sale, her radar pings, her eyes pop wide and I hear those dreaded words: "Let's stop for just a minute."

On our last trip, she was asleep when I noticed a sign for a flea market, so I sped up, hoping to sneak past.

I nearly got away with it. Then a voice from the passenger seat said, "Thought I didn't see that one, didn't you?"

—PAUL BRINKS

The speed limit is the maximum speed you can go by law and also basically the minimum speed you can go without ticking everybody else off.

—LORDPOUNCE ON REDDIT.COM

Joke's on you, kids who put shaving cream on my car. I was gonna shave my car anyway.

—@IBID78

When our car overheated in the middle of nowhere, the local tow truck driver hauled us into town, saying he was in a hurry. It was Good Friday, and everyone was going to the church for the Easter pageant. Despite being in a rush, the driver found the right thermostat for our car and fixed it. While he worked, we sat in his office with his wife and kids, who were growing increasingly impatient. His family was definitely late for church, but the driver shrugged it off.

"They can't start without me," he said. "I'm playing Jesus."

—MARY HACKETT

Amtrak tweeted this quote that allegedly came from a great poet: "Do not follow where the path may lead. Go instead where there is no path and leave a trail." User @porkbelt had this to say: "With all due respect, this is terrible advice for trains."

The driver I stopped for speeding insisted he had a valid excuse.

"Sorry, officer," he said. "I just had the car washed and was drying it out."

—CHARLES DUNNING

One of my chronically late employees showed up later than usual. At least he had a good excuse: "The train that gets me here 10 minutes late was 10 minutes late."

—PATRICIA JOHNSON

A co-worker at our auto auction was having trouble starting one of the cars.

Looking defeated, he complained, "The only thing that's working is the blinker on the check engine light."

—DENNIS MARQUADT

Call it kismet, but when a car thief near Portland, Oregon, took off in a Toyota Land Cruiser, it didn't take long for police to find him. That's because, minutes into his crime, the suspect crashed into a Buick Regal. The magical part? The other car also happened to have been stolen.

—KPTV.COM

I pulled over a 17-year-old for speeding. When I told him I'd clocked him at 101 mph, he insisted he was doing only 85.

"Why do you think that?" I asked.

He yelled back, "My speedometer only goes to 85, and I had the pedal pushed all the way to the floor!"

—POLICEONE.COM

As a teenager, my grandfather dreamed of having a horse. His father didn't understand why, but he reluctantly agreed to let my grandfather work in order to earn enough money to buy one. I have a cassette tape of my grandfather talking about his boyhood longing for a horse, of "the need to mount a steed and ride against the wind at full speed." To digitize this recording, I enlisted the help of my 16-year-old son. When we finished, my son asked, "Now do you understand why I want a car?"

—LORETTA EVANS

If the helicopter pilot asks if you like roller coasters, maybe think about why he'd ask that before you gleefully exclaim yes. I know this now.

—@ARCHETYPEANGEL

The longest drum solo was 10 hours and 26 minutes and was performed by the child sitting behind me on Delta Flight 963 from Los Angeles to Tokyo.

—@FAKEMUSICFACT

Salesman: This car has all the latest high-tech features. For example, if you get too close to another vehicle, this new car makes a loud beeping sound to warn you.

Customer: Big deal. My old jalopy does that as well. If you get too close to another vehicle, it makes a loud crunching sound.

—JEFFREY SCOTT HULE

Car trips with my wife are just great because I get to listen to 10 seconds each of 400 songs she hates.

—@DADDYGOFISH

One day, as a state trooper, I pulled over a young man for speeding. I sat in the front seat of my cruiser and began to write him a citation. He tried making small talk while he waited.

"It sure is a beautiful day," he said.

Without looking up, I continued to write. "Yes, it is," I said. "I wish I was fishing!"

He had the perfect response to that.

"No offense, sir," he said. "But I wish you were fishing too."

I laughed so hard, I let him go that day with just a warning.

—JOHN WARNER

***Cashier:** I think I know you from somewhere.*

***Customer:** I have a big following on Instagram.*

***Cashier:** Don't you work at the car wash over on Third?*

***Customer:** Yes. It could also be from there.*

—@REALOVERHEARDLA

The flight from Moscow to Irkutsk, Siberia, is a long one, so I was lucky to nab a window seat in an exit row. But as the Aeroflot jet gained altitude, I began to feel an icy draft on my legs and then noticed that the exit door was not properly closed. Alarmed, I pointed out the problem to a flight attendant. She promptly took care of the situation: She brought me a blanket.

—CECIL TAYLOR

Before flying to Fort Meade to administer a language proficiency exam, I wrote a packing checklist, which I then promptly managed to lose. When I arrived at my hotel room, I opened the suitcase and discovered that it had been searched by airport security.

How did I know, you ask? On the top of my clothes was my checklist. On the bottom of the list someone had scribbled: "You forgot your after-shave and your tester's manual."

—YEFIM M. BRODD

Rebranding "not knowing how to drive" into "climate activism."

—@LORIBERENBERG

Two hours into a flight, the pilot gets on the intercom.

"We just lost an engine," he announces. "It's all right—we have three more. But the flight will take us an hour longer." A half-hour later: "We just lost another engine. Don't worry; we have two more. It'll take us another two hours, though." In the back, an irritated passenger rolls her eyes.

"Great," she says to her seatmate. "If we lose the last two engines, we'll be up here all day."

—7THSPACE.COM

As my roommate drove me to work, I begged him to stop off at a diner. In a hurry, he begrudgingly pulled over. I jumped out and grabbed a coffee to go, and soon we were on our way again. But just as I was opening the lid to take a sip, he hit a large pothole, causing me to spill coffee all over myself.

"Didn't you see that pothole?" I yelled.

He replied tersely, "I hit it, didn't I?"

—JOHN CUFF

Being the youngest child means no matter how old you get, you're always going to be stuck in the middle seat of the car.

—@COCOTOOMAJIAN

"It's the guy behind us. He says his horn is broken."

While at a motel in North Dakota, I went to breakfast and sat by a gentleman who was on the phone. I overheard him say that he had "lost time yesterday" because his "passengers got cranky," so he "stopped at a truck stop and hosed them down with cold water." Then I noticed a school bus in front of the motel that hadn't been there the day before. When the gentleman ended his call, I asked him if that was his bus.

"No," he replied. "I'm in the back with a semi load of pigs."

—DAVID FLEMMING

I was a federal agent, interviewing a young man for his security clearance. I knew that he'd been arrested for speeding a few years earlier, but he hadn't said so on his application. When I asked him why, he said he didn't think the arrest counted.

"Why wouldn't it count?" I asked.

"Because I didn't have a driver's license."

—MIRIAM KITMACHER

A tip for road trips with kids: My 5-year-old hasn't said a word after I convinced him that the volume control on our stereo ejects his car seat.

—@BRIANHOPECOMEDY

We asked my Great-Aunt Luella how long it took for her and Uncle Campbell to drive the 125 miles from their home to ours.

"With no traffic, it takes about two and a half hours," she said. "But if there's a lot of traffic, it's only two hours, because Campbell has to pass everyone."

—CAROL PARKER

While carpooling, we pulled up to the driveway for our next passenger. We honked and waited, honked and waited, and honked again. Our co-worker finally came out.

"I'm so sorry I kept you waiting," she said, climbing into the car. "But I only heard the third honk."

—ELSIE WILLMS

Years ago, as a young man driving a very old station wagon, I was pulled over for speeding.

"You know, you were going 55 in a 45-mph zone," the officer said.

But I knew he was wrong and told him. "Honestly, Officer, I don't think this piece of junk can go that fast."

"You know, that's the best excuse I've heard in a long time." He then got back into his patrol car without ticketing me.

—ARNIE MAESTAS

Hundreds of Indian passengers were stuck aboard a train for two hours after the conductor abandoned his post. Turns out he was hot, so he went home to take a cold shower.

—INDIATODAY.IN

In his late 80s, my father-in-law went to the DMV to renew his driver's license. At one point during the road test, he approached a four-way stop, looked to his left and cruised straight through the stop sign.

"Sir! You didn't look to your right," yelled the frightened inspector.

My father-in-law calmly shook his head. "That's Mum's side."

—PATRICIA L. BUCK

Did you hear about the director of the Department of Motor Vehicles who resigned on Tuesday? He tried to resign on Monday, but he found he'd been standing in the wrong line.

—DAVE MARGOLIS

A state trooper pulled alongside a speeding car on the freeway. Glancing at the car, he was astounded to see that the elderly woman behind the wheel was knitting.

The trooper cranked down his window and yelled to the driver, "Pull over!"

"No!" the woman yelled back. "It's a cardigan!"

—KNITTINGHELP.COM

UFOs

It's funny they call them "unidentified flying objects." I could identify them right away. Those are UFOs.

—@DLICJ

If aliens ever attack, we will probably be fine unless they realize how easily we are influenced by traffic cones.

—@SEANFORHIRE

The first time I flew, there had been UFO sightings near Green Bay, Wisconsin. My plane made a stop there, and when we were back in the air, I noticed red and green lights following us. After noting this for several minutes, I summoned a flight attendant.

"I don't want to sound an alarm," I said, "but those lights have been following us since Green Bay."

She looked out the window, leaned closer to me and replied, "I hope so. Those are the wing lights."

—MARSHA ROBINSON LOOYSEN

"I happen to be a frequent flier, and this just doesn't feel right to me."

WARP

On our railway, children age 10 and under travel at half-price. As the conductor began checking tickets, a woman sitting next to me told her daughter, "Now remember, you are only 10." The girl nodded her head.

The conductor then approached them and asked the girl, "How old are you?"

"I am 10, sir."

"And when will you be 11?"

"As soon as I get off this train!"

—THEODORUS HARI WAHUANTO

My uncle only polished the front half of his car because it was the only part he saw when he drove it.

—@GALGOSRGREAT

After he finished his route, a bus driver had to explain to the supervisor why he was 10 minutes late: "I was stuck behind a big truck."

"But yesterday you were 10 minutes early," reminded the boss.

"Yeah," the bus driver replied. "But yesterday I was stuck behind a Porsche."

—TIM HARVEY

Living in rural Minnesota, I find driving through crowded Minneapolis difficult.

"I have trouble figuring out when to turn and what lane to be in," I complained to my grandson. His wife could commiserate.

"I understand," she said. "I never know which cornfield to turn at when we visit you."

—JANET KROGFUS

If you have a boat and a happy marriage, you don't need another thing.

—ED MCMAHON

One of my math students got his hand caught in a go-cart chain and lost a third of his finger. He missed a couple of days of class.

When he returned, I asked him if his injury hindered him in any way. But he was surprisingly upbeat.

"No, it actually helps me," he said cheerfully. "Now I can work fractions!"

—LARRY WEATHERS

On the shuttle bus headed from the Denver airport to the car rental area, I sat across from a man gazing out the window at the beautiful Rocky Mountains. A smile creased his lips as if he recalled a wonderful distant memory. He turned to his young son seated next to him.

"This is where I met your mother," he said.

His son excitedly yelled, "On this bus?"

—RHONDA NEAL

QUOTABLE QUOTES

THEY SAY YOU ONLY GO AROUND ONCE, BUT WITH A MUSCLE CAR, YOU CAN GO AROUND TWO OR THREE TIMES.

—TIM ALLEN

I saw a documentary on how ships are kept together. Riveting!

—STEWART FRANCIS

Admit it, sport utility vehicle owners! It's shaped a little differently, but it's a station wagon! And you do not drive it across rivers! You drive it across the Walmart parking lot!

—DAVE BARRY

In America there are two classes of travel—first class, and with children.

—ROBERT BENCHLEY

Thanks to the Interstate Highway System, it is now possible to travel from coast to coast without seeing anything.

—CHARLES KURALT

You're gonna need a bigger boat.

—*JAWS*

It puzzles me how they know what corners are good for filling stations. Just how did they know gas and oil was under there?

—DIZZY DEAN

Most people hate cellphone use on trains; I love cellphone use on trains. What do you want to do, read that report on your lap or hear about your neighbor's worst date ever?

—LIZA MUNDY

If you don't know where you are going, any road will take you there.

—LEWIS CARROLL

IF GOD WANTED US TO FLY, HE WOULD HAVE GIVEN US TICKETS.

—MEL BROOKS

A COUPE OF A DIFFERENT COLOR

That old clunker was ready to paint the town

By Martha Mahon

Money was scarce around our house with a family of 12 during the Great Depression. My parents made sure we had plenty to eat and a roof over our heads, but anything more than that, we had to pay for it ourselves.

My brother Frank was determined to get a car. So he worked in a grocery store every day after school and saved all his earnings for two years. By the time he turned 18, he had enough to buy his first car.

He was very proud of it and could not wait to show it off. With their first glance at it, my parents could feel their blood pressure soaring. It was a beat-up old coupe with a rumble seat and in desperate need of a paint job. Having spent all his savings to buy the thing, Frank had no choice but to use the paint that was left over from our bathroom and kitchen decorating—yellow and pink.

Mother had an anxiety attack whenever she looked at that yellow-and-pink eyesore parked in front of our house; the rest of us just tried to avoid the neighbors.

In spite of his car's paint job and condition, Frank always managed to get plenty of dates. I'm sure his good looks had something to do with it. And it helped that not many 18-year-olds had a car back then.

Occasionally, Frank would double-date with a friend, but because only two fit in the cab, the other couple had to ride in the open-air rumble seat and take their chances with the weather. I remember watching the four of them drive off one fine summer night without a cloud in the sky. Minutes later, a sudden thunderstorm drenched the unlucky pair perched in the rear.

I still laugh about that car.

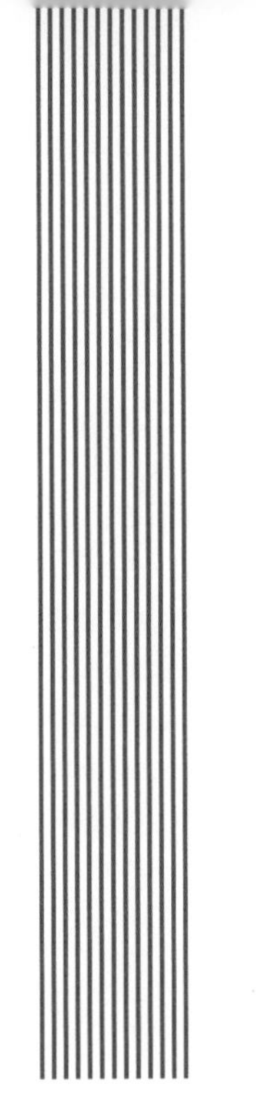

LET'S GET PHYSICAL

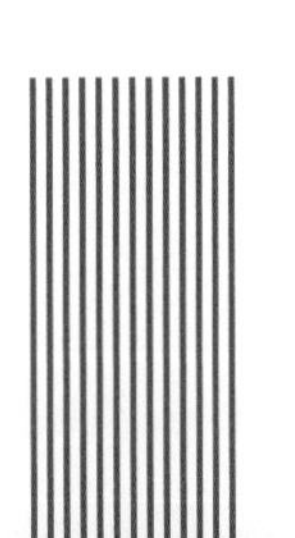

The score was close and the end of our volleyball game was near. I dived for a ball but pulled up when I saw another teammate already after it. She bumped it straight up in the air. I leaped to my feet but didn't know where the ball was. Suddenly, the ball hit me—no joke—square on top of the head. It arced up into a perfect set that another teammate spiked over the net. We won the point—and the game.

—SUSANNAH REAVIS

After one of his second grade flag football games ended in victory, our grandson asked, "If the NFL drafts me, do I have to go?"

—DALE SHOOK

About 10% of Americans fill out a March Madness bracket for a pool at the office or with friends. Here are some signs you won't be winning any prizes for yours:

- You think Gonzaga is a euphemism.
- Your top seed? Sesame.
- Your "Which mascot would win in a fight?" methodology yielded a showdown between the Long Island University Ninja Pirates and the Iona Chuck Norrises.
- Your Final Four includes the University of Phoenix and Hogwarts.

—HUMORLABS.COM

Tee Time

Golf is literally a sport to see who can play the least golf.

—21COSNER ON REDDIT.COM

Golf is the perfect thing to do on a Sunday because you spend more time praying on the course than if you went to church.

—BROCKOLI117 ON REDDIT.COM

As far as I can tell, the requirements to be a professional golfer are the same as to be a drag queen: crazy outfit, crazy name.

—@GABYDUNN

The average golfer walks about 900 miles and drinks 22 gallons of alcohol each year. Which means golfers get about 41 miles to the gallon.

—VENKMAN62 ON REDDIT.COM

The safest place to stand when I hit a golf ball is directly in front of me.

—@INKEDUPKIDDER

The part of the baseball game I most identify with is the umpire neurotically dusting home plate after the players mess it up.

—@AMYDILLON

I had joined an aerobics class made up mostly of older women like me. At first it was difficult to follow all the steps, but after a few weeks I felt that I had a good grasp of the routines. One day, a fellow classmate stopped me to say, "I've been noticing you. You're very coordinated."

I couldn't have been prouder.

"Thank you!" I said.

"Yes," she continued, "your shirt matches your pants, and your pants match your socks."

—JOYCE THOMASSON

You should be able to play defense at bowling.

—@GARFPOOOP

I played on a softball team with many rookies who'd never played before. One of my teammates hit a hard line drive. As she rounded first, we hollered, "Go to third!" And so she did—right across the pitcher's mound.

—GAIL VALENCE

Things I overheard at my health club:

- "I'm only taking this class so I don't eat for an hour."
- "Who knew 40 years of neglect would have repercussions?"
- "Does this body make me look fat?"

—MARK GARVEY

Doctor's orders say 30 crunches a day. That's an awful lot of chocolate, but I guess I can give it a shot.

—@WX388

When no one else stepped up, my husband volunteered to coach our son's soccer team despite having no knowledge of the sport. The boys went the entire season without scoring. Before the final game, one player told my husband, "At Sunday school this morning, I prayed to score a goal." That game, the team scored their first goal ever! But they still lost 2-1. That same player said after the game, "I guess I should've prayed to win."

—NANCY BEASLEY

At 5 feet, 10 inches and 114 pounds, our son, Dan, is the skinniest player on his high school football team. During one of his games, I remarked to a cousin, "I wonder why they gave him the uniform with the number 1 on it."

"It's probably the only one that fit," she said.

—DIANE FELDMAN

Our high school has lots of spirit, but that didn't help the football team, which had yet to win a game. So when our principal saw some cheerleaders sitting in the stands, he asked, "Don't you think you girls should be down there cheering for your team?"

"I think," one of them said, "we should be down there *playing* for our team."

—EMILY KARNES

Years ago, I joined a bowling league. My score rarely broke 100, but one night I threw a ball that popped out of the gutter and knocked down all 10 pins. I was thrilled to have gotten a strike—until my teammates told me it didn't count. When we had our awards dinner, I received an award for being the only person to ever get a gutter strike at that bowling alley. Even though it didn't count, I'd still done something no one else had.

—LISA HARRIS

My husband hasn't been to the gym in over a year. One day, I asked him to come with me.

"No," he said, "I need to lose a few pounds before I go back."

—SANDRA CURRAN

The Chinese Professional Baseball League played most of the 2020 season in empty stadiums, but the Rakuten Monkeys had a home-field advantage. Their owners stocked the seats with robots. If only they'd been programmed to lob heckles like these:

- "Hey, batter! You swing like your tension-amplification mechanism was sent to the wrong 3D printer!"
- "C'mon, let's score some runs! If I wanted to look at zeros and ones all day, I would've gone to work!"
- "ERR-OR! ERR-OR! Your suckiness at fielding does not compute!"
- "Look alive out there, team! You're the ones with consciousness, remember?"
- "These guys make how much money? They haven't even been programmed not to spit!"

—NEWYORKER.COM

One of my wife's third graders was wearing a Fitbit watch, which prompted my wife to ask, "Are you tracking your steps?" "No," said the little girl. "I wear this for Mommy so she can show Daddy when he gets home."

—JAMES AVERY

A golfer standing on a tee box overlooking a river sees a couple of fishermen and says to his partner, "Take a look at those two idiots fishing in the rain!"

—GREG LANG

When I was a student at Wake Forest University in North Carolina, I lived in a dormitory named after a famous alum, Arnold Palmer. A big portrait of the golfer hung in the foyer. One day, a friend of mine—an international student from China who didn't know who Palmer was—came to pay me a visit. When she got to my room, she asked me, "Why is there a huge painting of George W. Bush in the lobby?"

—E.G.

My 2-year-old son, Lucas, was determined to buy a new toy at the dollar store. We were waiting in line to pay for a carefully chosen set of toy golf clubs when Lucas announced, "Mommy, we forgot to get something!"

"What's that?" I asked.

"The hole!"

—CHARLYN BARRINGTON

Great news for a player on the Gateway Grizzlies, a professional baseball team in Sauget, Illinois: With his team losing 3–0, he cracked a grand slam to take the lead! Bad news for the player: The ball sailed into the parking lot and smashed his car's windshield.

—STLTODAY.COM

AN OPEN LETTER TO THE GUYS WHO KICKED THE SOCCER BALL OVER THE FENCE AND ASKED ME TO TOSS IT BACK TO THEM, THUS SCARRING ME FOR LIFE

For the sports-averse, an unexpected game of catch can feel like a penalty

By Jen Cordery

ear Guys Who Kicked the Soccer Ball over the Fence and Asked Me to Toss It Back to Them, Thus Scarring Me for Life,

I'd like to talk to you about the two minutes of sheer humiliation you subjected me to last night. Let me first refresh your memory: You, a group of fit young men, were playing soccer on the AstroTurf field across from my apartment building. I, a better-than-average-looking young woman, was walking by with my groceries, whining silently to myself about the pain the half gallon of milk was causing my nonexistent arm muscles. That's when your ball came flying over the fence and landed at my feet. One of you approached and asked politely if I would toss the ball back to you. Fighting the urge to flee screaming down the street, I agreed.

Before I continue, let me shed light on something that I didn't have a chance to mention last night: I hate sports. More specifically, I hate any sport with a ball. This stems from my lack of natural ability when it comes to throwing, catching and hitting. I'm bad at aiming, too, and also at general hand-eye coordination.

However, wanting to appear agreeable, I put my bags down, picked up the ball and, grimacing, eyes half shut, threw it as hard as I could.

It hit the middle of the fence and bounced back to me.

Trying to act oh-so-nonchalant, I chuckled and muttered something about being out of practice, then picked up the ball again. If you'll recall, at your behest, I agreed to try throwing underhand. I thrust the ball upward with all my might, thankful that your anticipatory applause stifled my involuntary grunt.

The ball hit slightly higher up on the fence and bounced back to me.

This is the point where I start to take issue with you. Wouldn't it have been a better use of your time, and mine, if you had just walked around the fence and retrieved the ball then? I was clearly struggling, and I had turned an unhealthy shade of scarlet. And yet you all just stood there, transfixed.

Seeing that you weren't going to let me off the hook, I became desperate. Mortifying memories of middle school softball came flooding back.

Being a big girl now, I pushed those memories aside and picked up the soccer ball for the third time. I forced a good-natured chortle while crying inside as you patiently lobbed words of support over the fence at me as if I was a 2-year-old holding an inflatable beach ball for the first time.

"Throw it granny-style!"

"Just back up a little and give it all you've got!"

I know you thought you were being encouraging, but it only served to deepen the humiliation.

Nevertheless, I accepted your advice, backed up, rocked back and forth a little, breathed in and let it fly.

It hit the rim of the fence and bounced back to me.

I willed myself to have a heart attack and pass out just so I'd be put out of my misery. Alas, the heart attack didn't happen, and you continued to look at me expectantly, as if you were content to do this all night. I had become a spectacle for you. I could feel your collective thoughts drifting through the chain link: Can she really not do it?

Unfortunately for you, three failed attempts at a simple task in front of a group of people in a two-minute period was just enough degradation for me for one night. I picked up the ball, approached the fence and grumbled, "Please just come get it."

And you did. And thanks to you, I resolved at that very moment to never throw anything ever again, except disdainful glances at people who play sports.

Sincerely yours,
Jen Cordery

I ran a 5K for charity. After the race, I wanted to see how my time ranked in my category of men ages 30 to 34. I was close to the bottom, which I chalked up to being 34—the other guys were simply younger. I was determined to rank higher the following year, when I'd be 35 in the 35 to 39 age bracket. But that year, I was mistakenly registered in the over 70 category—and finished fourth out of seven. I can't even win against guys double my age!

—JOE BALTHAZOR

My brother Nick was an excellent halfback, and my dad often volunteered to work the first-down chains during his football games. Our team was down and the clock ticking when Nick got the handoff and broke free of the defense, charging downfield. Everyone was on their feet cheering. Caught up in the excitement, Dad ran down the sideline alongside Nick holding the chain pole above his head, yelling "Go, son, go!" The poor men on the other end of the chain just let go and started cheering too. Nick scored and ran to Dad for a big hug. The referee shook my dad's hand, took the chain and politely told him his chain-holding days were over.

—JOSEPHINE EVERETT

For the exercise-averse, good news! Researchers say that a mere three seconds of resistance training a day could boost our biceps by 12%. Meanwhile, *The Week* asked its readers to name a workout regiment that requires the absolute minimum level of effort. Here are the best responses:

- "CrossSit"
- "AutoPilates"
- "Chairmaster"
- "Gluteus Minimus"
- "Diddly Squats"
- "Chilates"
- "Zzzzzumba"

Personal trainer: No pain, no gain.
Me: Deal!

—@ABBYCOHENWL

"I ran a half marathon" sounds so much better than "I quit halfway through a marathon."

—@RICKAARON

If I was stuck on a desert island with only one record, I would want it to be the record for being able to swim the farthest.

—@GUYENDOREKAISER

"I told you this was a rough hole!"

An exercise for people who are out of shape: Begin with a 5-pound potato bag in each hand. Extend your arms straight out from your sides, hold them there for a full minute and then relax. After a few weeks, move up to 10-pound potato bags. Then try 50-pound potato bags, and eventually try to get to where you can lift a 100-pound potato bag in each hand and hold your arms straight for more than a full minute. Once you feel confident at that level, put a potato in each bag.

—BEVERLY GROSS

Quick Quips

Do people who run know that we're not food anymore?

—@IAMENIDCOLESLAW

Our hometown baseball team is called the Possums. They get killed on the road.

—RICHARD KLIMKIEWICZ

Stop, Drop and Roll: A Beginner's Guide to Bowling

—@STEVIEKNIP

I don't want to exercise. I want to have exercised.

—@AKILAHGREEN

We get it, people on Instagram. You have enough clear floor space to do yoga.

—@BANANAFITZ

Anybody want to buy some exercise equipment? I'm having a going-out-of-fitness sale.

—@JOHNLYONTWEETS

Our son was upset that his baseball coach yelled whenever he or a teammate made a mistake.

"It's just something coaches do," I said. "It's not personal."

His response was hard to argue with: "If it's not personal, then why do they use your name?"

—LAURA MCKINNEY

Why do football players only dance when good stuff happens? Just once I wanna see a QB throw an interception and do a sad, interpretative dance.

—@MRGEORGEWALLACE

Sports analysts get paid to talk, not necessarily to make sense. Case in point:

- "I had a feeling today that Venus Williams would either win or lose."
—TENNIS COMMENTATOR MARTINA NAVRATILOVA

- "There's nothing wrong with the car except that it's on fire."
—RACING COMMENTATOR MURRAY WALKER

- "The wind is rushing from the player's rear."
—GOLF ANNOUNCER STEVE MELNYK

- "We haven't had any more rain since it stopped raining."
—TENNIS COMMENTATOR HARRY CARPENTER

—KATHRYN AND ROSS PETRAS IN *THE STUPIDEST SPORTS BOOK OF ALL TIME*

Pregnant with our second child, I was determined to ride my exercise bike at least 2 miles a day. Late one night, having put it off all day, I climbed aboard the noisy contraption in our bedroom, where my husband was reading a book. After about 20 minutes of listening to the squeaky machine, he glanced up, somewhat annoyed.

"Don't you think it's time you turned around and headed for home?" he asked.

—MARGARET KOCH

They call the Kentucky Derby the fastest two minutes in sports. But they haven't seen me start, then quit, a 5K.

—@BOBTHESUIT

Sandy began a job as a school counselor and was eager to help. One day during recess, she noticed a girl standing by herself on one end of a playing field while the rest of the kids enjoyed a game of soccer at the other end.

Sandy approached the girl and asked if she was all right. The girl said she was.

But a little while later, Sandy noticed the girl in the same spot, still by herself.

Approaching again, Sandy offered, "Would you like me to be your friend?"

"OK," said the girl, looking at Sandy suspiciously.

Feeling she was making progress, Sandy then asked, "Why are you standing here all by yourself?"

"Because," said the girl with great exasperation, "I'm the goalie!"

—COURSEHERO.COM

If I ever say the words "my fantasy football team," just know it is code for "I've been kidnapped please help me."

—@LAURABENANTI

SIDEWINDER SAM'S
AEROBIC STUDIO

My high school had a legendary basketball coach who retired just prior to my arrival. He still came to give us a pep talk before a big game against the best team in the state. He told us, "Those boys put their britches on the same way you do." Inspired by his wisdom, we went out on the court and got beat like a drum. I saw the coach in the lobby after the game. He smiled and said, "I probably should've told you their britches were a lot bigger and moved faster than yours."

—BOBBY HART

Saw some idiot at the gym put a water bottle in the Pringles holder on the treadmill.

—@MIKHANX

In honor of our armed forces, the University of South Carolina football team used the backs of players' jerseys to display a little patriotism. They placed words like *Duty, Service, Courage* and *Commitment* where players' names would normally go. During the game against the University of Florida, a fight broke out, prompting the television commentator to announce, "It looked like Integrity threw the first punch."

—MIKE GADEL

It can take a sports franchise years to build up a fearsome reputation—and just one word to tear it down. Jimmy Fallon asked viewers of *The Tonight Show* to add a word to ruin a team name. See if you could now root for the ...

- Chicago Care Bears
- Buffalo Unpaid Bills
- Los Angeles Toenail Clippers
- Denver Chicken Nuggets
- Minnesota Olsen Twins
- New York Stevie Knicks
- Los Angeles Phone Chargers
- Utah Jazz Hands
- Sacramento Burger Kings
- Golden Girls State Warriors

When I coached high school tennis, there were never enough courts, so people were always waiting to play. One younger player passed time by tossing his racket back and forth from hand to hand. After some time, he asked for my help finding something—his tooth, which he'd knocked out when he hit himself in the face with the racket. Players from both squads were on their hands and knees searching the grass. No luck. The player said, "That's OK, Coach. It was artificial. I knocked that same tooth out last year."

—WAYNE SANDERS II

HOCKEY TALK

Seven phrases that will help you sound like an expert

By Sophie Kohn

o apparently it's time for "the playoffs" to start up again. If this information fills your soul with purpose and joy, great! But if it makes you feel a creeping sense of dread as you brace yourself once again to be brutally excluded from every known social interaction, please voyage back in time several years with me to one particular office I worked at. Because I think I can help.

Seemingly every day once springtime began, there'd be a pause in our team meeting. The air in the room would shift. And I'd instantly know, on a cellular level, that the moment had arrived. I'd glance anxiously at the clock. Our lunch break was 6,000 hours away. Or just one hour. Same thing. My senses grew heightened. I was the arctic hare of this office, listening, twitching, awaiting the inevitable.

They'd all lean back in their chairs. Laptop screens pushed down, various body stretches executed. That was enough work, apparently. And then, sure enough:

"OK, what the hell was that game last night?"

It's impossible to overstate how passionate, and how constant, the hockey discussion was in this job. Unfortunately, I had nothing to contribute to any hockey conversation at any time, other than repeatedly shrieking "they play it during the Olympics!!"

One day I was venting my frustrations to a co-worker, Mike—a person who knows a ton about hockey while also possessing an acute awareness of how alienating the sports universe is to an outsider. I'd expected him to sympathize and ask which esophagus-destroying coffee kiosk in the basement food court we should give our hard-earned money to today.

Instead, he leapt straight into action as if he had been waiting his entire life to rescue someone trapped in an endless *Groundhog Day*-esque hockey conversation she was constitutionally unable to participate in.

"You need stock phrases," he replied with alarming immediacy. "Completely empty, meaningless sentences you can throw into any hockey conversation to sound like you're an authority."

He emailed me a list that day. And I deployed them constantly, with a barely contained and delirious joy. I'd shout one with my feet up on the table, loudly smacking my gum. Then I'd cut people off midsentence to shout another. I simply would not be stopped. I would be stared at and laughed at by my whole office, but I was too enamored of my new identity—a fun, opinionated person I named "Hockey Janet!"—to care.

In case you, gentle reader, ever find yourself in a similar predicament, I share these sacred phrases with you now. Wield them with gleeful abandon and enjoy the sweet new feeling of—what's this?—belonging.

1. **"They're just not moving the puck."** You don't need to know which two teams played; one of those teams failed to move the puck adequately.
2. **"He's really changed the culture."** At the first mention of a last-namey-sounding word—Tavares! Matthews!—fire this into the discourse. Was the name mentioned disparagingly? With awestruck reverence? There's no time for irrelevant details; buddy's changed the culture either way.
3. **"There's always next season."** Who can argue with this?
4. **"I'm worried about their depth."** Apparently the defensive line (that's right: I did actually pick up some real terms too) has to be a certain number of players deep to work optimally. Expressing fear about this not happening? Startling power move. Congratulations, you're now the undisputed Lord of the Conversation.
5. **"That guy has a real feel for the game."** It means literally anything. It also somehow means literally nothing.
6. **"Say what you want, but the schedule hasn't done them any favors."** If in doubt, you can always feel confident asserting that the players' punishing schedule is the reason for their failure to perform good hockey.
7. **"They've gotta start letting the game come to them."** What? I have no idea, but this instantly makes you sound like a revered hockey commentator with nine municipal parks named after you, and that's all that matters here.

I signed up for a Zoom workout class that was too advanced. So when the instructor said, "Do a plank and bring your knee to the opposite elbow," I did a modified version where I turned off my computer and made pancakes.

—@MORGAN_ MURPHY

After my daughter sat glued to the TV set for most of the day, I told her, "Do you know that the average American spends more hours per day watching TV than the average Olympic athlete spends training?" She replied, "What's the point of all that training if no one's going to watch?"

—DAVE KOLACZ

My 9-year-old grandson Michael wiped the sweat from his face while taking a quick break from his soccer game. The coach ordered him back on the field.

"I'm so tired," Michael moaned.

"You're too young to be that tired," the coach countered.

"Well," Michael persisted, "I'm 63 in dog years."

—COLLEEN LACHNER

I coached my son's Little League team. We lost every game until the last. In the final inning, we were in the field, ahead by 1 with no outs and the bases loaded. The batter hit a line drive right to our third baseman. She stuck out her glove with one hand and covered her eyes with the other. The ball landed in her glove. She jumped up and down, stomping on third base to make the second out. Then she stuck out her glove to show me the ball, tagging the runner coming in—an unassisted triple play! Our team ran to the pitcher's mound in celebration as if it were the World Series.

—ROBERT DROZEL

My daughter and her friend played on the high school basketball team. My daughter usually started, while her friend spent more time on the bench. One night, they burst through our front door. My daughter yelled, "I scored 20 points!" Her friend yelled, "And I jumped up and down a lot!"

—SUSAN SHELLEY

"Something's wrong. He's never walked this far before."
—What my shoes would say if you walked a mile in them

—@IBID78

"If I get dizzy and pass out, there's a cherry Danish in my lunchbox."

THE ABDOMINAL SNOWMAN
WEYANT

On a brutally humid day, I walked past a miniature golf course and saw a dad following three small children from hole to hole.

"Who's winning?" I shouted.

"I am," said one kid.

"Me," said another.

"No, me, me!" yelled the third.

Sweat dripping down his reddened face, the dad gasped, "Their mother is."

—TOM LAPPAS

The person who came to my office looking for work was a former Los Angeles Dodgers minor league baseball player. On his résumé was this reason for leaving his previous job: "Couldn't hit a curveball."

—KENNETH P. MULDER

My husband bought an exercise machine to help him lose weight. He set it up in the basement but didn't use it much, so he moved it to the bedroom. It gathered dust there, too, so he put it in the living room. Weeks later, I asked how it was going.

"Well," he said, "I do get more exercise now. Every time I close the drapes, I have to walk around the machine."

—PHYLLIS OLSON

I remember being at girls' high school volleyball games as a little kid and thinking "These are some of the most powerful babysitters in the world."

—@LOUISVIRTEL

Honestly, my biggest fear about becoming a zombie is all the walking.

—@GASHLEYMADISON

I am an 84-year-old gentleman who stands 5 feet, 4 inches tall, from the basketball-crazy state of Indiana. Recently, my wife and I were having dinner at a local restaurant. Our waiter was a young man, around 6-foot-8. Naturally, I asked him if he played basketball. He looked down at me, replied, "Yes, I do," and then asked me if I played miniature golf.

—PAUL KINGHORN

Before my 7-year-old daughter's softball season started, I told her I wanted her to do two things: Have fun and get one player out. As the season was ending, she'd had a blast but she hadn't made an out. Finally, a ground ball was hit to her, and I yelled, "First base! First base!" She stood and made a perfect throw—to second base. When she got back to the dugout, I asked why she threw to second. She said, "Dad, when I looked up, second was the first base I saw."

—SCOTT BURKS

QUOTABLE QUOTES

WHY DOES EVERYBODY SING "TAKE ME OUT TO THE BALL GAME" WHEN THEY'RE ALREADY THERE?

—LARRY ANDERSEN

My New Year's resolution is to get in shape. I choose round.

—SARAH MILLICAN

You want proof baseball players are smarter than football players? How often do you see a baseball team penalized for too many men on the field?

—JIM BOUTON

Jogging is very beneficial. It's good for your legs and your feet. It's also very good for the ground. It makes it feel needed.

—CHARLES M. SCHULZ

Watching soccer is like watching grass grow, with soccer players in the way.

—STEPHEN COLBERT

Swimming is a confusing sport, because sometimes you do it for fun, and other times you do it not to die.

—DEMETRI MARTIN

Anyone who's just driven 90 yards against huge men trying to kill them has earned the right to do jazz hands.

—CRAIG FERGUSON

Whenever I feel like exercise, I lie down until the feeling passes.

—ROBERT HUTCHINS

I think foosball is a combination of soccer and shish kabobs.

—MITCH HEDBERG

I'm so unfamiliar with the gym, I call it James.

—CHI MCBRIDE

CROSS-COUNTRY SKIING IS GREAT IF YOU LIVE IN A SMALL COUNTRY.

—STEVEN WRIGHT

A BIRD IN THE HAND

When they tell you to ride the ostrich, you learn to wing it

By Judy Pearce

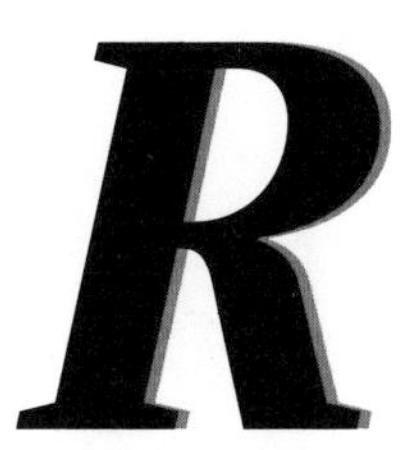

acing ostriches was the half-time entertainment at the Channel City Horse Show in Santa Barbara, California, in 1963. The birds' owner had brought them to the showgrounds with the understanding that the manager would drum up some volunteers crazy enough to ride them. I was one of the people he called.

As I waited to enter the arena, a farrier offered some alarming advice. "Those guys kick out to the side, so you'd best stay behind them. Last week I saw a bird kick in the wheel of a Porsche with one strike."

I began to fear that some great harm might befall me, but it was too late to back out. Half a dozen ostriches were waiting for riders. I marched into the ring with the other fools.

The stands were packed. My bird was struggling with two stewards who were holding it by a leather strap.

"Hurry up," one steward hollered, "we can't hold it much longer. Just grab the strap and jump on!"

Turned loose with greenhorn riders, the birds were whipped into a racing frenzy by a cowboy on horseback, who yelled and waved a broom with zealous glee. I'm a longtime equestrian, but the gait of a two-legged creature is decidedly different. It bobs back and forth, and left to right. Luckily, I kept my grip!

We'd arranged ahead of time for a steward to pass me an ostrich egg in secret after I dismounted, which I managed with difficulty. When my bird squatted, I casually slipped the egg under it. Laughter erupted when the ostrich stood up again.

The whole gig was a success, with birds and riders receiving a standing ovation. Shortly after that show I learned I was pregnant. For months, my husband joked, "I don't think she's pregnant. I think she caught something from those darn ostriches."

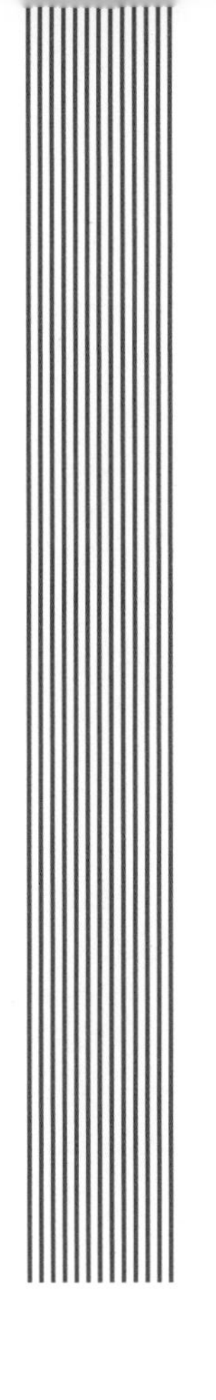

FASHIONABLY FUNNY

Wanting to look my best for the office party, I splurged on a new dress, strappy high-heel shoes and, to add a fashion statement to my newly pedicured toenails, a toe ring.

That evening, I sashayed into the club, head high, and approached my boss's wife. Pointing to my painted, bejeweled toes, I asked, "Notice anything?"

"Yes," she gushed. "That's quite a bunion you have."

—ZOE SCHREIBMAN

Clearly I was not going to win the battle of the bulge on my own, so I decided to join a gym.

"Before you start working out, we would like to do a health assessment," explained the gym representative. "When you come in, wear loose-fitting clothing."

"If I had any loose-fitting clothing," I told her, "then we wouldn't be having this conversation."

—KELLY BLACKWELL

A teenager waltzed into our jewelry store to buy a cross for her boyfriend. I showed her a selection, and she pointed to three: "Can I see that one, that one and the one with the little man on it?"

"Oh," I replied. "You mean Jesus?"

—JULIE SWARSBRICK

My 5-year-old grandson was looking through some old photos when he noticed his grandfather in his Marine dress blues.

"Grandpa, what kind of costume is that?" he asked.

"That's not a costume," my husband growled. "Men have died for that uniform."

The boy looked up and said, "So you stole it, then?"

—ARLETTA LEHR

We waited in line to enter the Space Mountain ride at Disney World alongside a woman and her young son. The boy wasn't tall enough to go on the ride, but his mother had a solution. She took a pair of high heels out of her backpack and forced him to wear them.

—BUZZFEED.COM

Saw a police officer dressed as a pilot today and thought it was weird. Then I realized he must be one of those "plane clothes cops."

—@TMONEY68

My father dragged my brother Scott to the barber to get his beautiful long hair shorn. Arriving at the barbershop, Scott asked to use the bathroom. He went in, and Dad and the barber waited. And they waited, and waited. Finally, Dad stormed into the bathroom, only to discover the window open and my brother nowhere to be seen. I never did find out how he got home.

—SHARON KEMP

Before heading out to the office, I asked my 8-year-old daughter, "So, do I look OK?"

She looked me up and down before giving me the thumbs-up and saying, "Not as bad as you did yesterday!"

—BARB LEE

My sister and I were working in our parents' store when we caught two women stuffing baby clothes into their large purses.

"That's it," they said indignantly as they threw the clothes on the counter just before storming out. "Under no circumstances will we ever shop in your store again!"

—LAURIE SANCHEZ

While I was applying face cream, my husband asked my daughter what I was doing. She yelled back, "She's applying Oil of Delay."

—MJ ROBARTS

When I was in my 20s, I had a streak of gray hair. One day, a complete stranger noticed and said, "I really like your gray hair. Where did you get it done?"

"Oh, thanks," I said. "It's natural."

She recoiled. "Oh my, what are you going to do about it?"

—DONNA CALVERT

Tracia and Patrick Kraemer met at a nudist park and fell in love. "It was our third date before we saw each other dressed. And that was a good thing," Tracia said, addressing Patrick, "'cause had I seen you dressed on the first date, I probably wouldn't have dated you again. You wore those two different brown plaids together; that was terrible."

—NPR.ORG

Attending our church's Christmas program, I noticed that many men there had full beards. Knowing my wife's aversion to facial hair, I teasingly whispered to her, "How do you think I'd look with a beard and mustache?" She whispered back, "Lonely."

—ROBERT C. BAPTISTA

As I welcomed my first grade students into the classroom, one little girl noticed my polka-dot blouse and paid me the ultimate first grader's compliment: "Oh, you look so beautiful—just like a clown."

—PRISCILLA SAWICKI

A woman saunters out of the bedroom modeling a lovely garment.

"Look at this!" she says to her husband. "I've had it for 20 years, and it still fits."

Her husband nods. "It's a scarf."

—D. GOLIGHTLY

My 13-year-old nephew thought his "gangsta" outfit—low-riding pants and exposed boxers—made him look cool. That is, until the day his 5-year-old cousin took notice.

"Nathaniel," she yelled out in front of everyone. "Your panties are showing."

—LINDA MCLEMORE

"I think I'm getting gray hairs," I told my husband. "But I can't be sure, because my eyesight isn't what it used to be."

My optimistic spouse replied, "Sounds like it's all working out fine!"

—CINDY SMITH

TEN MINUTES BEFORE THE INVENTION OF THE HAIRCUT.

A New York matchmaking service has launched "Smell Dating," which allows users to choose potential mates by sniffing swatches of their unwashed T-shirts. *The Week* asked its readers to title a romantic comedy about an aromatic couple:

- *You've Got Smell*
- *The Musk of Zorro*
- *Soapless in Seattle*
- *Bridget Jones's Laundry*
- *When Harry Sniffed Sally*

Sometimes I worry that my 9-year-old is too sweet for this world, but recently she looked at my face and said, "I didn't know you could be old and get a pimple." So it turns out she'll be fine.

—JESSICA VALENTI

A man rushed to the jewelry counter in the store where I work soon after the doors opened one morning and said he needed a pair of diamond earrings. I showed him a wide selection, and he quickly picked out a pair. When I asked him if he wanted the earrings gift-wrapped, he said, "That'd be great. But can you make it quick? I forgot today's my anniversary, and my wife thinks I'm taking out the trash."

—ANDRE F. PAYSON II

Save money by just buying bigger pants instead of paying for a one-year gym membership.

—@ENVYDATROPIC

After his first day back at school in the fall, I asked my son if the high school students were wearing anything new.

"Well," he replied, "a lot of the fellows are showing up in see-through mustaches."

—BEATRICE W. COLVIN

I think we can all agree that hairdressers are the unsung heroes for looking at the pictures of celebrity hair we want and not laughing in our faces.

—@IHIDEFROMMYKIDS

Why do baby clothes have pockets? Are people really going up to babies and saying, "Hey, can you hold this for a second?"

—@Y2SHAF

As I was stepping into the shower after a day of yardwork, my wife walked into the bathroom.

"What do you think the neighbors would say if I cut the grass dressed like this?" I asked.

Giving me a casual glance, she replied, "They'd say I married you for your money."

—JOHN R. BUCO

My brother recently ran into a woman he'd gone to school with many years earlier. After they caught up, she showed him a picture of her daughter.

"Wow," he said. "She doesn't look anything like you. She's pretty."

—CINDY EARLS

I only use shampoo that smells like raspberries so people don't think it's weird when I have jam in my hair.

—@DAWN_M

My wife and I were at the circus watching a shapely young woman dangling from a trapeze. The woman appeared to be wearing a very revealing costume, and my wife exclaimed, "There's nothing underneath!"

At first I agreed, but studying the woman more closely, I saw there was flesh-colored material under her costume. So I said, "No, there's flesh-colored material underneath."

My wife replied, "I meant there is no net underneath the trapeze. What were *you* referring to?"

—THANE LAFOLLETTE

Spiffy Spectacles

I bet when the first guy wore glasses everybody was like "Oh la-di-da, excuse me Mr. I Need TWO Monocles."

—@ROBFEE

When one girl finished the English portion of the state exam, she removed her glasses and started the math questions.

"Why aren't you wearing your glasses?" she was asked. She responded, "My glasses are for reading, not math."

—KATHY OLSON

My husband's new "unbreakable" titanium eyeglasses broke. When he brought the many pieces back to the optometrist to have the glasses replaced, the assistant asked what had happened.

"They fell under the lawn mower," he explained.

"Oh," she said, nodding. "Were you wearing them at the time?"

—SUSAN STRONG

"What's a hipster?" asked my 4-year-old cousin.

"Someone who will wear something just to look different," I said. "They'll often buy clothes in thrift shops and wear thick glasses."

"Is Grandma a hipster?" he asked.

—EYESHA SADIQ

SALE
REDUCED
FOR
CLEARANCE
Galef
McConnell

THE INVENTION OF THE MIRROR

Once a year our church group holds a sale to raise money for its youth group. At our last sale, just as we finished putting everything out, a middle-aged man arrived in a huff. Growling, he yanked two sports coats and a few suits off the rack, then stomped over to the cashier, where a puzzled volunteer asked if everything was all right.

"I don't know what the world is coming to," the man said in an injured tone. "This is the third year my wife has donated my favorite clothes to this church sale!"

—MAGGIE THEISS

While shopping in India, I asked the store owner for any locally made yarn. The merchant brought down a skein that was clearly marked "Made in China." I pointed it out, but he insisted I was wrong.

"Oh no," he assured me. "Only the label was made in China."

—JANE GELMAN

I was at the customer-service desk, returning a pair of jeans that was too tight.

"Was anything wrong with them?" the clerk asked.

"Yes," I said. "They hurt my feelings."

—A.P.

During a lesson about adjectives, my friend, an elementary school teacher, asked her class to describe their mothers. One boy described his mother's hair as auburn. Impressed by his sophisticated word choice, my friend asked, "How do you know her hair color is auburn?" Her student replied, "Because that's what it says on the box."

—JOAN ANASTASI

I was standing in the grocery checkout line, wearing the shirt my wife had given me for my recent birthday. It read: "I am the square root of 4,900 years old." The lady in line ahead of me turned around and looked at it, then said, "I have no idea what that means." The young man at the next register explained, "Ma'am, that means he is 700 years old!"

—FRED SALLEE

A man snatched the cash drawer from a church gift shop in Florida, took off and was pursued by a church worker, who might not have caught up with him except that the thief's oversize pants slipped down around his ankles—and tripped him.

—REUTERS

THE PERFECT SALON? A BARBER SHOP

When it comes to the perfect hairdo, some salons just won't cut it

By Patricia Pearson

I **had my** hair cut in a barber shop the other day. I know that's a bit unusual for a middle-aged woman, but I finally just refused to fork over 10 times as much money as my husband pays to have shorter hair.

I've always been envious of the way Ambrose impulsively acquires a cheap buzz cut as casually as he buys batteries at the corner store. My son is the same. "Less hair, please. Thank you." And that's all there is to it.

Though it took me weeks to pluck up my courage, at last I walked into Enzo's Hairstyles for Men in Toronto as if I had every right to be there. No appointment necessary.

It was a plain room full of old vinyl chairs and stacks of sports magazines. Enzo nodded at me courteously when he spied me on a chair in the waiting area. When he didn't seem surprised by my presence, I realized it was all about my confidence: To finally be free of women's salons, all I had to do was get over the fact that I'd walked into a barber shop for men.

For years, I have found going to salons to be a deeply tormenting experience. I have very straight, fine hair, and less of it now that I'm in my 50s. There is nothing I can do with it. Unless your cheekbones are apparent, and you have a piquant little chin like Audrey Hepburn, this kind of hair is going to be the bane of your existence no matter how much you spend on it.

When I was younger, I thought it was a matter of finding the just-right stylist. Every few months, I'd walk into a different salon with fresh hope and check in with a receptionist who had a way of making me feel like a lost cause because, well, just look at my hair!

These salons would make me don a cranberry-colored robe, like when you get a CT scan. Then, stripped of whatever personality I could project through my fashion choices, I'd discuss cuts with the stylist, as if any of the models in the hair magazines look like a typical middle-aged woman.

I'd get escorted to the sinks to be lathered with specialty products, even if I'd washed my hair that day, and then for the next hour, the fashionable stylist would clip microscopic strands from all over my head while engaging in awkward chit-chat.

"So, what do you do?"

"I'm a writer."

"Oh, cool."

Silence.

"Would you like me to put in some amber and russet highlights?"

I knew this would take hours and cost more than my heating bill.

"No, thank you."

Silence.

Then, invariably, I'd exit with a head of hair that looked as good as it ever would, knowing that the second I washed out the conditioner, mousse and spray that had propped it up like meringue, it would go back to looking like it did before. My salon visits felt increasingly delusional.

But I soldiered on. At one point, when my two kids were little, I heard about hair extensions that could add volume. This was exciting. I spent hundreds of dollars and several hours to have them meticulously weaved in. The result was amazing.

Guess what happened next? My children came home from school with lice. Lice! I then got infested and had to return to the salon to have the extensions removed.

Finally, years later, my eureka moment. Hello, Enzo's!

Here, the walls were festooned with soccer posters. A tinny radio played old hits. Enzo, who smoked as he worked, wore a pale yellow shirt and light gray pants. He could as easily have been a hardware store clerk.

He was using a straight razor to shave a young man dressed in black; a starving artist, I thought, perhaps scribbling away at a novel. A burly fellow waiting his turn wore a grease-stained T-shirt—maybe a mechanic. The last thing these three men had in common was any interest in style.

When my turn for a haircut came, I hopped into one of Enzo's worn barber chairs. "Take 2 inches off, please," I announced.

He swiveled the chair away from the mirror, calmly combed my mid-length hair, and snipped. It took five minutes. Cost very little. Looked just fine. Praise the Lord.

"Well, you won't find old-style guys like Enzo for much longer," warned Ambrose when I came home pleased with my freshly trimmed hair. "Now it's all fancy young types with waxed mustaches who try to turn you into a hipster. I just might start going to a women's salon."

Former football star and TV personality Michael Strahan is known for his gap-toothed grin. But on the "Mean Tweets" segment of *Jimmy Kimmel Live!*, Strahan read aloud a tweet from someone who is clearly not a fan: "Michael Strahan's teeth are having a middle school dance, where the boys stand on one side of the room and the girls stand on the other."

Jennifer's wedding day was rapidly approaching, and she was horrified to learn that her mother had bought the exact same dress for the wedding as her father's young new wife. Jennifer implored her stepmother to exchange hers, but she refused. So Jennifer's mother agreed to buy a different dress for the wedding.

"Are you going to return the other dress?" Jennifer asked. "You really don't have another occasion where you could wear it."

Her mother smiled and said, "Of course I do, dear. I'm wearing it to the rehearsal dinner the night before the wedding."

—FRIARSCLUB.COM

For my Sunday sermon, I purposely buttoned my suit vest incorrectly to illustrate how hard it is to fix things once you've started out on the wrong foot. So I stood before my congregation, opened my suit coat and asked, "Does anyone notice anything unusual about me?"

A child shouted, "Yes, your shoes are dirty."

—LEWIS KUJAWSKI

What my girlfriend thought, first four dates:

Nice shirt.

Wow. A second nice shirt.

OK, first shirt again.

He has two shirts.

—@RISTOLABLE

The topic of conversation was nose jobs. My slightly confused young daughter asked, "Where does the doctor get the new noses to replace the old ones?"

"They have a place that manufactures them," I answered. "It's called the 'olfactory.'"

—WAYNE EGGLESTON

If I ever voiced disapproval of a photo of myself, my mother always had a ready reply: "Want a better picture? Get a better face."

—MARIA ZAGORSKI

DRESSING ROOMS
NOW WITH DIMMER SWITCHES
Sale

Not to brag, but my son's friend said "Your dad looks hot" when I was cleaning the pool. She followed with "Is that heatstroke?" but still.

—@THEBOYDP

Back when my daughter was an infant, I was out pushing her in the stroller when a woman stopped us on the street.

"My goodness, what a beautiful baby!" she remarked. "Does she look like her father?"

—PEGGY GREB

As the hostess at the casino buffet showed me to my table, I asked her to keep an eye out for my husband, who would be joining me momentarily. I started to describe him: "He has gray hair, wears glasses, has a bit of a potbelly ..."

She stopped me there. "Honey," she said, "today is senior day. They all look like that."

—ROSALIE DARIA

As any Southerner knows, there's nothing quite like a backhanded compliment from a proper southern lady. Here are some favorites from the Alabama-based website *al.com.* Y'all feel free to borrow them:

- "I just love how you don't care what people think. That takes a special person."
- After you tell her you lost 9 pounds: "Well, that's a wonderful start."
- "I bet those shoes are comfortable."
- After you arrive for a visit: "What'd you do, sugar, drive all the way here with the windows down?"
- "I bought this the other day, but it's too big on me. Do you want it?"

As I continue to go bald, every day is both the worst hair day of my life and best hair day I'll have for the rest of my life.

—REDDIT.COM

"My hair's not messy. It's on an adventure."—My 9-year-old daughter, officially kicking off her career as my spiritual advisor

—@LETMESTART

A friend is someone you can text "Do I look good in yellow?" and three dots appear and disappear twice before you get back "No."

—@BESSBELL

Ah, married life. While shopping for vacation clothes, my husband and I passed a display of bathing suits. It had been at least 10 years and 20 pounds since I had even considered buying a bathing suit, so I sought my husband's advice.

"What do you think?" I asked him. "Should I get a bikini or an all-in-one?"

"Better get a bikini," he replied. "You'd never get it all in one."

—GCFL.NET

I realized my 17-year-old son was spoiled the day he called to his mother, "Ma, are the clothes in the dryer clean?"

—PAUL MILLARD

Quick Quips

Why is it called a *dad bod* and not a *father figure*?

—@SKINNERSTEVEN

"Pull over! Now get out of the car slowly and let me see your shoes." —Fashion Police

—@LISABUG74

I'm sick of men's 3-in-1 bodywash-shampoo-conditioner. Throw toothpaste in there.

—@COMRADTWITTY

Haircuts are great because I did none of the work but get all of the credit.

—@LUDWIG

Not sure who this "dry-clean only" shirt thinks it's dealing with.

—@OHNOSHETWITNT

What do you call a tailor who only alters pants? *A slacker*.

—@THUGRACCOONS

Lice was detected on a student at my grandson Ryan's school, and the teacher told the girls in Ryan's first grade class to wear their hair in a bun to discourage the lice. Needing clarification, Ryan asked, "A hot dog bun or a hamburger bun?"

—PAULINE KETTLEBOROUGH

Dry shampoo is the equivalent of unicorn blood for hair—it'll keep it alive, but it'll be a half life, a cursed life.

—@ELLIEPEEK

Eleanor Roosevelt once said to "do one thing every day that scares you." Today, I'm going jeans shopping.

—@JAKE_40K

In one of his last interviews, Eddie Money, the late musician and star of AXS TV's reality show *Real Money*, admitted to *Rolling Stone* that his wife didn't like how he appeared on screen.

"My wife says to me, 'You look heavy on TV.' I said, 'Honey, the camera adds 10 pounds.' She said to me, 'How many cameras did they use?'"

I wish days-of-the-week underwear were still a thing so I would know what day of the week it is.

—@LHLODDER

When the box with my Halloween costume arrived, it was empty. I called the company and asked where my Maid Marian costume was.

"We're sorry, ma'am. We'll send you the costume tomorrow," the representative said. "In the meantime, please feel free to keep the Lady Godiva costume you got by mistake."

—KAREN ATANASOFF

"It's the shower drain again."

When my friend's husband was deployed, he often sent her romantic and flirty gifts. One day, a package arrived containing a very small leather top. After much wiggling and squirming to get into it, she struck a pose, took a selfie and sent it to him. Soon after, she received his reply: "Why are you wearing the steering wheel cover I sent you?"

—KATHY TRUMAN

My 7-year-old stares at my face.

Me: What is it, sweetie?

Seven: Is my nose weird too?

—@THISONESAYZ

With fire alarms blaring at my mom's apartment complex, she grabbed her favorite bathing suit and ran out.

"A bathing suit?" I said later. "Of all the priceless things in that apartment, that's what you chose to save?"

"Material things come and go," she said. "But a one-piece suit that doesn't make you look fat is impossible to replace."

—CATHY PEACOCK

Halfway through a romantic dinner, my husband smiled and said, "You look so beautiful under these lights." I was falling in love all over again when he added, "We gotta get some of these lights."

—SHAWNNA COFFEY

When my mother did her laundry on a sunny day, she liked to hang her wash on a clothesline in the backyard. I was on the phone with her when an unexpected shower popped up. She said to me, "I have to go. It's starting to rain, and I have to go outside and take off my clothes."

—SANDRA YOUSE

Male teachers at my old school had to wear suits. But one colleague always managed to subvert the dress code by wearing the ugliest ties. Every day, staff and students alike couldn't wait to see what hideous accessory he had on. When he retired, I finally asked him, "Why the ugly ties?

He responded, "Because that way, no one would ever know I only owned one suit."

—ROD HANSON

I work with kids, and I'd recently gotten my hair cut. A little boy named Jaiden asked, "Miss Joanne, did you get a haircut?" Trying to be funny, I replied, "I got 'em ALL cut." He looked at me quizzically and asked, "What's a mall cut?"

—JOANNE RIVERA

QUOTABLE QUOTES

I WILL BUY ANY CREME, COSMETIC OR ELIXIR FROM A WOMAN WITH A EUROPEAN ACCENT.

—ERMA BOMBECK

If men can rule the world, why can't they stop wearing neckties? How intelligent is it to start the day by tying a little noose around your neck?

—LINDA ELLERBEE

She got her looks from her father. He's a plastic surgeon.

—GROUCHO MARX

I think the most important thing a woman can have—next to talent, of course—is her hairdresser.

—JOAN CRAWFORD

Where lipstick is concerned, the important thing isn't color, but to accept God's final word on where your lips end.

—JERRY SEINFELD

I base my fashion taste on what doesn't itch.

—GILDA RADNER

A celebrity is anyone who looks like he spends more than two hours working on his hair.

—STEVE MARTIN

I have mixed emotions when I receive my Father's Day gifts. I'm glad my children remember me; I'm disappointed that they actually think I dress that way.

—MIKE DUGAN

I was going to have cosmetic surgery until I noticed that the doctor's office was full of portraits by Picasso.

—RITA RUDNER

I BUY EXPENSIVE SUITS. THEY JUST LOOK CHEAP ON ME.

—WARREN BUFFETT

LOST AND FOUND

Sometimes misplaced belongings turn up where they're least expected

By DeLila Lumbardy

For years, I had to wake up long before the sun rose and drive 35 miles to work. I'm retired now, but I still wake up early and start each morning with an invigorating shower.

Most days, I wear comfortable leggings and baggy sweatshirts. I lay out what I'll be wearing on the edge of my tub the night before so that my outfit is ready to go after my shower.

One recent morning, though, I encountered a problem. After showering and drying off, I was ready to get dressed, but I couldn't find my underwear anywhere.

This struck me as strange. I'm a creature of habit, and I always lay my undies on top of my other clothes since they're the first thing I put on. Also, I could remember taking them out of the drawer—I could even remember which pair I'd chosen.

I shook out my leggings and my sweatshirt to make sure they hadn't gotten stuck in the folds of fabric. I turned out the pockets of my robe. I even peered into all of the drawers and cupboards in my bathroom. But they weren't there. And I was the only one in the house, so I knew that I wasn't the butt of someone else's practical joke.

Eventually, I gave up and retreated to my bedroom to pull a new pair from my dresser. As I slipped one leg in and then the other, I realized that something was off, and I glanced down to identify the problem.

I was already wearing underwear. I must have put on the pair that I'd originally chosen immediately after getting out of the shower!

I didn't know whether to laugh or cry, but I've heard that people who are able to laugh at themselves tend to live longer than those who take themselves too seriously. Hopefully that means that I'll be around for many more years!

D’OH!

To enter our closed community, one needs to punch a few numbers on a keypad. When my son was visiting, he asked for the code.

"It's the year that Columbus discovered America," I told him.

A few minutes later, my son, who, I should state, is the CEO of a thriving corporation, called to say, "Dad, the gate won't open, even though I keep pressing 1776."

—C.J. MULER

Upon finding a clearly plagiarized paper, I called the offending student into my office. Pointing to my computer screen, I said, "I found your entire paper online. Do you have anything you want to say about that?" Her angry response: "Well, I paid my sister to write it, but I didn't think she'd plagiarize!"

—CHRISTINA M. RAU

At a boat rental concession, the manager spots a boat out on a lake and yells through his megaphone, "Number 99, come in, please. Your time is up." Several minutes pass, but the boat doesn't return.

"Boat number 99," he again hollers, "return to the dock immediately, or I'll have to charge you overtime."

"Something's wrong, boss," his assistant says. "We only have 75 boats."

The manager pauses, takes a second look, and then raises his megaphone: "Boat number 66, are you OK?"

—MARINISTE.LIVEJOURNAL.COM

Recently, while walking with a friend, I stumbled and fell hard onto the pavement. Luckily only my pride was hurt, or so I thought. I brushed myself off and kept on going.

The next morning, while walking into the bathroom, everything was blurry and fuzzy. Looking into the mirror made me even dizzier. Fearing that I had a concussion from the fall, I panicked.

Then I realized I had put on my husband's glasses instead of my own. What a relief!

—MARGE JESBERGER

Teacher: What's the age difference between the two brothers in the story we read?
Student: Do you want to know the age difference at the beginning of the story or at the end?

—BLANCHE DOSS

"You're right. We should have built the castle first, THEN the moat."

As a Scottish police officer drove around Glasgow during her night shift, she noticed a bright light in the sky—likely a drone—following her. She tried evasive maneuvers, but it kept tracking her. Unnerved, she returned to the station, where a senior officer explained that the drone was actually the planet Jupiter.

—*DAILY RECORD*

Louis Angelino is a professional cleaner. A new client texted him the address and said the key was under the mat. Angelino arrived, found the key and got to work. After three hours of mopping and scrubbing, he was done. Just then, his client called asking where he was.

"I'm in your living room playing with your cats," said Angelino.

"Louis," said the client, "I don't have cats." And that's how Angelino learned that he'd broken into a stranger's home and cleaned it for free.

—NJ.COM

A guy tells his psychiatrist, "I always have this weird dream where I'm locked in a room. There's a door, but no matter how hard I try to push it open, it won't budge.

"Interesting," says the psychiatrist. "And does it say anything on the door?"

"Yes!" the guy replies. "It says Pull."

—GCFL.NET

"You're Lucky, Dave. You have talent."

NOT-SO-DUMB JOKES

Some jokes just make you chuckle, and thank goodness for them. But some punchlines make you stop midlaugh and actually think.

By The Javna Brothers

An elderly woman is watching her grandson play on the beach when a huge wave sweeps him out to sea. Frantic, she drops to her knees and pleads, "Please, God, save my only grandchild. Bring him back to me!"

Suddenly another wave comes in and delivers the boy onto the beach, as good as new.

The grandmother looks up to heaven and shouts, "He had a hat!"

In other words ... Don't be a jerk. A little gratitude goes a long way.

Sherlock Holmes and Dr. Watson go on a camping trip. After a good dinner and a bottle of wine, they retire for the night. Some hours later, Holmes wakes up and nudges his faithful friend. "Watson, look up at the sky and tell me what you see."

"I see millions of stars."

"And what do you deduce from that?"

Watson ponders for a minute, then says, "Well, astronomically, it tells me that there are millions of galaxies and potentially billions of planets. Astrologically, I observe that Saturn is in Leo. Meteorologically, I suspect that we will have a beautiful day tomorrow. Theologically, I can see that God is all-powerful and that we are just a small part of the universe. But what does it tell you, Holmes?"

"Watson, you idiot!" Holmes says. "Someone has stolen our tent!"

In other words ... Hey, genius: Smarts aren't always a substitute for common sense.

One evening over dinner, a boy asks his father, "Dad, are bugs good to eat?"

"That's disgusting," said the father. "You know the rules! We don't discuss things like that at the dinner table."

After dinner, the dad asked, "Now, what was it you wanted, son?"

"Oh, never mind, Dad," the boy

said. "There was a bug in your soup, but now it's gone."

In other words ... If you get stuck on following the rules, you might learn things the hard (and crunchy) way.

A doctor walks into the examining room and pats his patient's shoulder.

"I'm afraid I have some bad news. You're dying, and you don't have much time left."

"Oh no!" says the patient. "How long do I have to live?"

"Ten," says the doctor.

"Ten?" cries the panicked patient. "Ten what? Days? Weeks? Months?"

The doctor calmly replies, "Nine ..."

In other words ... Life is short—and getting shorter every day.

"See that kid?" a barber says to his customer, pointing to a boy standing outside the shop. "He is the dumbest kid in the world. Watch. I'll prove it to you." The barber takes out a one-dollar bill and a five-dollar bill, then calls the boy inside. He holds out both bills and asks, "Which one do you want?"

The kid takes the one-dollar bill and leaves the shop.

"See?" the barber says, laughing. "The dumbest kid in the world."

The customer leaves the barbershop and spots the boy coming out of an ice cream store. He says, "If you don't mind my asking, son, why didn't you take the five-dollar bill?"

The boy takes a lick of his ice cream cone and says, "Because the day I choose the five, the game is over."

In other words ... A fool and his money are soon parted. Just be sure you know which one of you is the fool.

It was Black Friday, and there was a big sale at the electronics superstore. People lined up outside at 5 a.m. At about 7:30 a.m., a short guy in khaki pants tried working his way to the front of the line. He didn't get very far before the mob grabbed him, wrestled him out of line and threw him into the parking lot.

The little guy soon got up, brushed himself off and tried again. He was barely able to take another step before an even bigger mob attacked him. The guy got up and started limping toward the front of the line a third time.

"Are you nuts?" asked one of the red-faced mob members. "Don't you know you're just gonna get tossed out of line again?"

"Yeah, I know," the man replied. "But if you don't let me get to the front of the line, I'll never be able to open the store."

In other words ... Your mother was right: Just because everyone else is doing it doesn't mean you should be too.

A man is driving home from work when his wife calls him on his cell phone.

"Phil!" she shouts in a panic, "Please be careful! I just heard that some lunatic is driving the wrong way on Route 80."

"You won't believe it, Doris," he replies. "It's not just one car; it's hundreds of them!"

In other words ... Sometimes there is a reason everybody's doing it one way. (Yes, Mom, we hear you!)

After weeks of rain, a town flooded and residents had to be evacuated. At one house, rescue workers found a man standing waist-deep in water. "C'mon! Get in the boat!" the rescuers shouted.

The man shouted back, "No! I have faith in God, and he will save me!"

Soon the floodwaters chased the man to the second floor. Luckily, though, another boat came by. "Get in the boat!" the rescuers urged.

"No way!" the man said. "I have faith in God, and he will save me!"

The floodwaters continued to rise, and the man had to climb to the roof of his house. Fortunately, a rescue helicopter came by and dropped a ladder for him. The pilot shouted through a megaphone, "Grab the ladder!"

The man refused. "No! I have faith in God, and he will save me!"

The floodwaters soon rose above the roof. The man was swept away and drowned. When he arrived at the Pearly Gates, he demanded an audience with God. "God," he said, "I was certain that you would save me. Why did you abandon me?"

God replied, "What do you mean? I sent you two boats and a helicopter!"

In other words ... If you hold out for a gift tied up with a bow, you might miss the present right in front of you.

A guy takes his date to a dinner at the local country club. It's an unusual setup: People have to wait in separate lines for each item on the menu.

As his date sits down, the guy volunteers to go get their dinner. First he waits in the line for the roast beef. Then he waits in the line for the potatoes. Then he waits in the vegetable line, the bread line, the salad line and the gravy line.

Finally he brings back two heaping plates of food. "Are you thirsty?" he asks his date. "What would you like to drink?"

"A glass of punch would be nice," she says. So the guy goes to get it. He finds a line for wine, a line for beer, a line for soda and even a line for milk. After considering all his options, he gives up and returns empty handed.

In other words ... Sometimes there is no punch line. Know when to walk away.

I was in the nail salon when a woman in her 40s walked in and smiled at me. I couldn't place her, but she did look familiar. I'm active socially—I thought maybe I knew her from one of the groups I've joined. It was eating at me, so I caught her eye and said, "I think I know you. Maybe from an organization we both belong to?"

Smiling, she leaned over and whispered, "I'm the mayor."

—MARGARET WEBSTER

A husband and wife are playing a trivia game.

"How did you know there are seven rays on the Statue of Liberty's crown?" she asks.

"Easy—the seven original colonies!"

—GCFL.NET

My neighbor was on a mission trip to South America, so his wife attended a dinner party alone. When the woman seated next to her asked her why her husband hadn't come along, my friend explained, "He's been on the Amazon for four days."

The woman was impressed. "Really? Whatever is he buying?"

—VALERIE CHILDRESS

I used to run into this one guy at the coffee shop who never could remember my name. To prod his memory, I pulled out a dollar and said, "My name is Bill, just like this one-dollar bill."

"Got it," he said. A few days later, our paths again crossed. This time he gave me a big, confident greeting: "Well, hello, George!"

—BILL CRAFT

My wife and I like to take walks down the quiet roads in our small town. One day, we noticed a key on the road and hung it on a fence where a deflated birthday balloon had settled. We hoped that eventually someone would spot their missing key. A week later, we realized that our shed key was missing. We searched and searched, but it was nowhere. Then a lightbulb went on. Luckily, the remnants of that colorful balloon helped us spot it. We took it home for a test. Sure enough, we had lost and found our own key!

—RON EDGINGTON

Just bumped into a mannequin and said, "Sorry." Then said, "Oh, I thought you were a person." Then realized I was still talking to a mannequin.

—@AJBROOKS

During a drive through farm country, my mother spotted a large sign that made her shake her head: Orchard for Sale.

"Well, that's dumb," she said.

"Why do you say that?" I asked.

"Who's going to want to transplant all those trees?"

—LINDA THROP

I was on a business call when I realized I was late for a class at the gym. I must have sounded rushed, because the woman on the phone said, "Am I keeping you from something?"

I replied, "I have to leave for tai chi."

"Oh, wow," she said, sounding intrigued. "What country is that in?"

—LINDA PLATT

Quick Quips

I told my mom that I did a report on Mary, Queen of Scots, and she said, "She ruled Ireland, right?"

—@JJBID20

Just tried a coat on in T.J. Maxx. It was the coat of a customer trying on another coat.

—@LITTLECHIEF1982

I work at a museum, and a woman asked me if mummies were older than dinosaurs.

—PLEASEFIREME.TUMBLR.COM

The thing I hate most about daylight savings is getting up at 2 a.m. to change the clock.

—BRADFORD BOYLE

What do you mean I didn't win? I ate more wet T-shirts than anyone else.

—@PEACHCOFFIN

A Swedish mother wanted to have the name of her 2-year-old son tattooed on her arm. Although Kevin is not a particularly complicated name, the tattoo artist managed to misspell it by adding an *l*, turning it into "Kelvin." The mother was horrified. But after learning it would take multiple treatments to remove the tattoo, she and her husband came up with a far simpler and less painful fix: They changed their son's name to Kelvin.

—CTV NEWS

Scene: First-year Spanish class

Student: "So a bull would be *un toro*, right?"

Teacher: "Correct."

Student: "Then a female bull would be *una tora*?"

Teacher: "Um ..."

—AMANDA DUMMER

A little old lady had just returned home from an evening church service when she was startled by an intruder. As she caught the man in the midst of robbing her home, she yelled, "STOP! Acts 2:38!" (That's the one that goes "Repent and be baptized, in the name of the Lord, so that your sins may be forgiven.") The burglar stopped dead in his tracks. The woman calmly called the police to explain what she had done. As the officer cuffed the man to take him in, he asked the burglar, "Why did you just stand there? All the old lady did was yell scripture."

"Scripture?" replied the burglar, stunned. "She said she had an ax and two .38s!"

—ELDEROPTIONSOF TEXAS.COM

Redditors reveal the dimmest bulbs they've encountered:

- A woman I know bragged on Facebook that she scored 84 on her IQ test. She thought it was out of 100.
- I had a guy proudly tell me that he could write with his left and right hand equally well. He said it was because he was "amphibious."
- Toward the end of the movie *King Kong*, my then-girlfriend asked, "Is this based on a true story?"

A classmate was examining my driver's license. She seemed surprised when she noticed that it indicated that I was an organ donor. So much so that she asked, "Which organ did you donate?"

—@LEXADELGAY

I wrote "William Shakespeare (1564–1616)" on the whiteboard, and a sixth grader asked, "Is that Shakespeare's real phone number?"

—WEARETEACHERS.COM

Though my last name is not long, it can be confusing. So when a receptionist asked for it, I tried simplifying matters by saying "It's the first four letters of *suggest*." She smiled. "And how do you spell that?"

—DEB SUGG

"May I make a suggestion?"

Escape rooms are a popular craze where participants solve puzzles and clues to free themselves from a locked room. Many people find them fun, but not one Vancouver, Washington, burglar. After-hours, he broke into an escape room and became trapped. He eventually figured out how to leave: He called 911.

—RAVEMOBILE SAFETY.COM

I can't do small talk. I just asked the lady cutting my hair what she does for a living.

—@MOMJEANSPLEASE

My colleague's daughter called him at work to ask for help on a school project: a timeline of her life. He was glad to help, but it went off the rails with the very first question: "Dad, when did I start walking?"

He answered, "Walking to where?"

—LISSETTE CUADRA

Peanut allergies are nothing to sneeze at, and one mother whose son is highly allergic wasn't taking any chances. She called 911 after opening an Amazon package at home that was filled with peanuts—packing peanuts.

—PEOPLE.COM

Helplessness is defined by slipping a dollar into the office vending machine, only to watch your Twix get stuck on the coils. That's what happened to an Iowa man. But unlike the rest of us, he had a forklift at his disposal, which he used to jostle the machine until it freed his booty. He was fired the next day.

—*DES MOINES REGISTER*

The people of Plover, Wisconsin, wanted the name of their village writ large on the local water tower. So crews began painting. When they finished, travelers from near and far could now see that they were entering the picturesque village of "Plvoer." The locals commemorated the gaffe with a T-shirt that proclaims "I Lvoe Plvoer."

—KXAN

Haven't you heard there are no dumb questions in business? From these HR queries, that truism is clearly not true.

- "I falsified my résumé. Now that I'm working here, can I change it?"
- "Can my supervisor require me to have specific working hours?"
- "Can I have my salary deferred until next year so I don't have to pay taxes this year? I don't need the money this year."
- "Since my mother and father both died before I came to work at this company, will I be credited for bereavement leave I didn't have to take?"
- "Will you give me a raise if I stop smoking marijuana?"
- "Can I wear a swimsuit and towel on casual day?"
- "Every day my supervisor tells me to stop chatting and get back to work. Can he do that?"

—WORKFORCE.COM

This Twitter alert from the sheriff's office in San Miguel, Colorado, leaves no stone unturned: "A large boulder the size of a large boulder is blocking the southbound lane of Highway 145. Expect delays."

My co-worker asked the tattoo artist to draw the Chinese character for "free" that he found using a translation app. Turns out, it was very close to being accurate, but not quite. His new tattoo actually reads "tax free."

—BOREDPANDA.COM

"I keep writing 'Stone Age' instead of 'Bronze Age' on all my checks."

Actual things grown-ups have had to have explained to them, as shared on reddit.com:

- Why a room below sea level on a cruise ship would not have a balcony.
- In regard to the North and South Poles, that neither is "the one that is always hot."
- That Halloween has never—and will never—fall on Friday the 13th.
- That islands don't tip over if you put too much weight on the edge.
- That there are more than six bones in the human body ... she thought it was head, back, arms and legs.
- That Earth has one moon. The new moon on the calendar every month confused her.

Just before our chemistry exam, my two friends bet on who would do better. The one with the worse grade would owe the other one 14 chicken sandwiches.

"There's no way I lose this bet," said my first friend. "This test is heavy on math, and I always do well on math problems."

My other friend countered, "Fine. Double or nothing—24 sandwiches!" Guess who won the bet.

—SAMUEL THOMAS

One of life's great pleasures is to watch two idiots agree on something and then hear one of them say "Great minds think alike."

—@REALSUDONIM

Daughter (via text): Mom, where are you??

Mom: Leaving Walmart. Halfway home. Why, sweetie?

Daughter: You brought me to Walmart with you ...

Mom: OH, DARN! Be there in a bit!

—SPOTLIGHTSTORIES.CO

"Wordle" to the Wise

It hurts my feelings when Wordle hits me with "Phew!" when I get it on the last try.

—@COLLEEN_EILEEN

You're on Wordle. I'm on my 30th attempt to guess my own password.

—@SILICONE_ANGEL

The most embarrassing thing about Wordle is that when I don't get it in three, I am convinced I am about to learn a brand-new word, and then it's like ... THOSE.

—@C_GRACET

QUOTABLE QUOTES

THINK OF HOW STUPID THE AVERAGE PERSON IS AND REALIZE HALF OF THEM ARE STUPIDER THAN THAT.

—GEORGE CARLIN

I'm not offended by all the dumb blonde jokes, because I know I'm not dumb ... and I also know that I'm not blonde.

—DOLLY PARTON

Aristotle was famous for knowing everything. He taught that the brain exists merely to cool the blood and is not involved in the process of thinking. This is true only of certain persons.

—WILL CUPPY

Common sense is not so common.

—VOLTAIRE

It has yet to be proven that intelligence has any survival value.

—ARTHUR C. CLARKE

If you think education is expensive—try ignorance.

—DEREK BOK

One man alone can be pretty dumb sometimes, but for real bona fide stupidity, there ain't nothin' can beat teamwork.

—EDWARD ABBEY

He may look like an idiot and talk like an idiot, but don't let that fool you. He really is an idiot.

—GROUCHO MARX

Few people think more than two or three times a year; I have made an international reputation for myself by thinking once or twice a week.

—GEORGE BERNARD SHAW

SOME PEOPLE DRINK FROM THE FOUNTAIN OF KNOWLEDGE, OTHERS JUST GARGLE.

—ROBERT ANTHONY

INSECT INTERRUPTION

A craft project gone awry leaves one mom bugging out

By Karen Troncale

One winter morning, I bundled up my kids so we could gather pine cones in the woods. It was our first Christmas in our new home, and I thought a nature craft—glittery red-and-green pine cones—would be a perfect project.

At the edge of the woods, pine trees had dropped cones all over the ground. We began filling our baskets.

"Don't they smell good?" I held one to my nose. The kids did the same.

"Oh, Ben, don't taste it!" I grabbed the pine cone from his 2-year-old hand and dropped it in his basket. "Put them in here."

Once back inside, we spread sheets of newspaper across the kitchen table.

"Can I use the glitter now?" asked 4-year-old Jennifer, wide eyed.

"First we have to kill the bugs," I said.

"Bugs?"

"Yes. The pine cones might have bugs hiding out in them. Some people put them in the oven to kill them. But I think the microwave will be quicker."

I put a plate full of pine cones in the microwave and turned it on.

Staring up at the window, Jennifer suddenly asked, "Mommy, what's happening?" I turned and looked. Dozens of insects were scuttling across the glass. Panicking, I turned off the microwave and opened the door.

It was something out of a monster movie. When the pine cones got hot, hundreds, maybe thousands, of bugs crawled out of them, attempting to escape the heat.

Fighting the urge to either vomit or faint, I yanked the plate out of the microwave and ran to the door to set it outside—and I tossed the rest of the cones out there, too. Then I quickly vacuumed out the microwave.

"Mommy," said Jennifer, her little face crumpling. "Does this mean I can't use the glitter?"

"Of course not," I said, taking a deep breath and pulling out some construction paper. "We'll just make glitter-covered paper chains instead."

10

HUMOR
IN UNIFORM

A young airman showed up at formation needing a shave. When I asked why he hadn't taken care of that before he arrived, he complained, "Somebody moved my piano."

"Why would moving the piano cause you to miss shaving?" I asked.

His reply: "My razor was on the piano."

—ROBERT RHODES

A month into my stint in the Army, I was assigned to guard prisoners. The fact that I was very raw was made abundantly clear to me the first time I accompanied an inmate to the military prison. After we walked side by side for a few feet, the prisoner, who had a few years on me, pointed to my weapon and said, "You know, you should really walk behind me and have your rifle ready to fire in case I try to escape."

—HOWARD HEIN

During our introduction to Vietnam, the instructor warned us about the deadly sea snakes in the South China Sea.

"If one of those snakes bites you," he said ominously, "you'll take three steps and drop dead."

A newly arrived GI raised his hand and asked hopefully, "What if we stand still?"

—DICK CRISLIP

Marching in basic training, an Air Force cadet was constantly getting reamed out for watching the planes flying overhead instead of keeping his eyes forward. Finally, the instructor had had enough and devised an apt punishment. For the rest of that day, the cadet had to stand on the edge of the training area and wave to every plane that flew past, shouting, "Bye-bye! Have a safe flight!"

—TASKANDPURPOSE.COM

A few good military truisms:

- Need to find an officer ASAP? Take a nap.
- Army food: the spoils of war
- If you see a bomb-disposal technician running, try to keep up with him.

During basic training at Fort Dix, New Jersey, I was sent to the firing range to qualify as a marksman. After taking a few shots, I asked my sergeant how I'd done. "Son," he told me, "you better learn to use a bayonet real good."

—EDMOND KRYSZ

A buddy and I were discussing where to go camping when a man nearby interrupted.

"Guys," he said, "I was in the Army for 26 years. The last thing I'd want to do with my weekend is go camping! I have a boat that I take out on a lake and relax."

My pal chimed in, "I was in the Navy for 30 years. The last thing I'd want to do is be on the water!"

"I can relate," I said with a self-deprecating smile. "After 20 years as an Air Force officer, the last thing I'd want to do with my weekends is be on a golf course."

—CHRIS MORTENSON

Nebraska is a landlocked state, but that hasn't stopped it from having its own Navy. In 1931, the governor went on vacation and left Lt. Gov. T.W. Metcalfe in charge. "Governor" Metcalfe took full advantage, creating the Great Navy of the State of Nebraska to reward his friends with the title of admiral. Why? Who knows. The title came with no pay or responsibilities—did we mention that Nebraska is landlocked? Today, admiralties are handed out to people who have helped promote Nebraska, including Bill Murray and Bill Gates.

—*MILITARY TIMES*

As a young trainee, I was ordered to hand out the .30-caliber ammunition to the other guys. One catch: There was enough for only one bullet per person. As I handed the single bullet to the machine gunner, he nonchalantly held the cartridge aloft and asked, "Do they want me to fire this all at once?"

—CHARLES PETTY

While serving in South Korea, I was assigned guard duty. The ensign issued me a gun and a whistle, but I quickly realized there were no bullets. Brandishing the empty weapon, I asked, "What do I do if I run into trouble?"

The ensign replied, "That's what the whistle's for."

—GORDON STANLEY

Our platoon officer was a tough-talking woman who barked orders right and left. We referred to her as The Witch behind her back—or at least we thought it was behind her back.

One day, she approached a private on cleanup duty. As he came to attention, some water from the bucket he was holding spilled onto the platoon officer's shoes. She let the soldier wallow in fear before asking, "Did you really think I would melt?"

—MICHAEL BARRY

THOMAS
CAMOUFLAGED
FIRING RANGE

B**asic training** requirements while at Fort McClellan included a demanding 12-mile march. We got started at 6 a.m. and were pumped up for the trek. An hour later, drenched with sweat and feeling the heavy load of our packs, we wondered whether the end would ever come.

"Men," our sergeant yelled, "you're doing a fine job. We've already covered 4 miles!"

Revitalized, we picked up the pace.

"And," continued Sarge, "we should reach the starting point any minute now."

—GCFL.NET

At the Marine Corps Officer Candidates School, an instructor told us how all the physical training they would put us through would come in handy once we left the service.

"When we get through with you," he said, "you should be able to whip any civilian in a fight. And if you can't do that, you can surely outrun him."

—DAVID NELSON

I**t's not** news that seasoned Marines like to have fun with newbies. I had just landed on mess hall duty when my sergeant ordered me to double-time it over to another mess hall on base, ask for a much-needed item and bring it back, pronto. After he told me what it was, I ran off, eager to fulfill my mission. When I arrived, I repeated my order to the sergeant in charge: "I'm here to pick up 3 feet of salad bar."

It took a while before I realized what they were laughing about.

—LOREN DAWSON

A**s part** of my U.S. Naval Reserve requirements at Emory University's dental school, I attended a talk about proper dental procedures following nuclear warfare. Evidently, one of my classmates found the talk less than stimulating and fell fast asleep. Unfortunately for him, our lecturer caught him. Sidling right up to the unsuspecting student, the speaker shouted in his ear, "What would you do for a patient in the event of a nuclear war?"

My classmate sat bolt upright and responded, "Place a temporary filling, sir!"

—R.H. SASSER JR., DDS

D**riving on** the German autobahn for the first time, we kept passing signs for Einfahrt and Ausfahrt. "Those must be huge cities," I said to my sergeant.

He politely explained, "*Einfarht* and *Ausfahrt* are German for entrance and exit."

—DAVID KINNETT

An Army buddy and some other raw recruits were waiting to be sent on detail. As the officer in charge read off their names, each soldier jumped up and left the room for their new station, except for a guy named Jones. The officer called out, "Jones ... Jones ..." but no one answered.

After he'd called all the names, there was still one soldier left.

"Are you Jones?" the officer asked.

"Yes," the soldier replied, happy to be recognized. "But everyone I know calls me Bubba."

—RICK SAGE

Quick Quips

Q: Why do Norwegians put barcodes on their battleships?

A: So when they dock, they can Scandinavian.

—CSGO_KRIPTONAS ON REDDIT.COM

Whoever named them missiles wasn't very optimistic.

—@FRO_VO

During the war my granddad survived mustard gas and pepper spray. He's a seasoned veteran.

—VETERANLIFE.COM

"Son, when the Marine Corps wants you to have a wife, you will be issued one."

—MARINE CORPS LT. GEN. LEWIS "CHESTY" PULLER (1898-1971) TO A MARINE WHO ASKED PERMISSION TO BE MARRIED

When my Air Force wing deployed to Norway, our first sergeant wanted to make sure we behaved ourselves and blended in with the locals.

"You men are representing your country and the United States Air Force," he told us. "Remember, when in Rome, do as the Romanians do."

—JIM VIZE

My 6-year-old son and I were watching soldiers parading through our small town. Among the marchers were military police officers wearing armbands with "M.P." emblazoned on them. I asked Michael, "Do you know what those letters stand for?"

"Yes," he said. "M Portant."

—TONY TAYLOR

ALLEY OOPS

Office workers at a Navy base are a little too eager to let the good times roll

By Camille Engeldt

hen I was 18 in the late 1950s and living in New Jersey, I landed a job at the Bayonne Navy Base. I worked in an office building under the command of a very handsome—and very serious—naval captain.

Building No. 82 had offices opening off a long central corridor that ran the entire length of the building. One Friday after the captain left for the day, his secretary, Joan, passed around word that she could roll a bowling ball down the entire—considerable—length of the hall.

At the specified time, all 50 of us workers left our desks and gathered to witness the stunt. From all the excited chatter, you might have thought we were giddy teenagers rushing out of our classrooms on the last day of school. We lined the hall outside our offices after posting a lookout at one end of the corridor. At the opposite end, Joan eyed the projected path; then, with a mighty heave, she let the bowling ball rip.

Just at the moment the heavy ball left her hand, our lookout screamed, "Captain's coming back!"

In seconds, the hall was cleared of the dozens of spectators, who all scurried back to their posts.

Waiting in our offices, most of us never got to see the captain's face when he reentered the building. But I've always wondered what he thought. Was he alarmed by the sight of that ball hurtling toward him down the deserted corridor? Was he bowled over?

All we know for sure is that the captain carried the ball back to his office, where Joan sat typing. Somehow he knew the bowling ball was hers, and without a word he placed it on her desk. As he turned away, his face showed a hint of a smile.

Military newbies often find their gullibility preyed upon by pranksters who outrank them. Case in point: While serving on the USS Turner Joy, a naive young sailor came rushing into our supply office with an important requisition order that came straight from his chief.

"I need," he said, "a fallopian tube."

The storekeeper, remarkably keeping a straight face, asked, "What size?"

"I don't know."

"Go find out."

—RICHARD E. ASCHE

The technician taking my blood at the military medical clinic was very chipper, explaining, "I leave the service in two months!" As he applied the tourniquet around my arm, he assured me that the procedure wouldn't hurt much and then asked what my husband did in the service.

"He's a recruiter," I said.

"Hmm," he said wryly. "This might hurt more than I thought."

—GCFL.NET

During basic training, our drill sergeant often led us in a game of Simon Says to help teach us the marching commands.

"I bet you can't get me out," a private insisted.

Challenge accepted, the drill sergeant went through the commands, sometimes beginning with "Simon says" and sometimes not. The private was as good as he claimed and stayed in the game until the sergeant commanded, "Simon says, jump up!" The private leaped into the air and landed again.

"You're out!" the sergeant shouted. "Simon said jump up, but not down!"

—THOMAS WEBER

I asked a new trainee when he needed to hand in his paperwork.

Trainee: The training manager said any time after a thousand.

Me: A thousand? A thousand what? A thousand clicks? A thousand minutes?

Trainee: That's all her message said. See?

[Shows me the message, which does indeed say "After 1000"]

Me: OK, that's ten-hundred, as in, 10 a.m.

—NOTALWAYSRIGHT.COM

I asked my dad, a Navy guy, how far from land his ship was while on the ocean. "We were always just a few miles from land," he said. "Straight down."

—PAUL TRUSH

"In his spare time, Milton dabbles in foreign policy."

The U.S. Strategic Command detects and deters foreign attacks. So last year, when it tweeted ";l;;gmlxzssaw," the Twittersphere went into overdrive. Had StratCom been hacked? Was it a coded message? Neither. The Command's Twitter manager was working from home when he stepped away from his computer. His young son found the open Twitter account and sent his first tweet.

—*OMAHA WORLD-HERALD*

My third grader's teacher assigned the following prompt to the class: "Veterans Day honors the men and women who have served in our armed forces. Do you think you would like to serve in the military one day? Explain."

Here is Justin's response: "Yes, I would like to serve in the military someday. I would like to serve chocolate chip ice cream, strawberry, chocolate and vanilla ice cream. I would ask, 'What kind of flavor would you like?' I'd also ask, 'What kind of cone do you like?' That's what I would like to serve in the military."

—ADEL DIORIO

Deserved or not, the Air Force has the reputation of being the country club of the military service, as this joke will attest:

A commander asks some troops, "If you found a scorpion in your tent, what would you do?"

Army said, "Stomp on it."

Marines said, "Eat it."

Air Force said, "I'd call the concierge and ask why I had a tent in my room."

—VETFRIENDS.COM

The service is known for meting out creative punishments. Here are just a few, as witnessed by Redditors:

- After being caught staring at a squirrel while in formation at Officer Candidate School, one candidate was tasked with saluting every single squirrel he saw until he graduated.
- I saw a guy forced to slow dance with a mop for one hour.
- After someone screwed up on the firing range, our drill instructor made him face the mirror and yell, "You're stupid!" "I'm not stupid; you're stupid!" "No, I'm not stupid; you're stupid!" I think at some point the kid really thought he was arguing with himself.
- We made a private sweep the sunshine off the sidewalks.

At a reunion for my husband's Air Force bomber squadron, a man stood staring at me for the longest time. Finally, he came up to me and said, "I've got who it is you remind me of. I can't remember her name, but she was on *The Golden Girls*."

"Oh, the little grandma?" I asked.

"No," he said. "The dumb one."

—M.S.

When the sergeant told our new commander that his driver could not participate in an upcoming field maneuver because she was pregnant, the enraged commander demanded to know just how pregnant she was.

The sergeant's reply: "Completely, sir."

—DAVID RASBERRY

While in paratrooper training school, I asked the instructor, "What happens if the parachute doesn't open?" "It's guaranteed," he reassured me. "If it doesn't open, just bring it back."

—RICHARD HOFFMAN

After our physical, a sergeant addressed us draftees.

"I see you all are from a county that makes moonshine," he said. "Do any of you make moonshine?" Nobody answered.

"Do any of you drink moonshine?" Silence.

"Good, because the Army wouldn't have you if you did."

From the back: "Well, umm ... I drink a little."

—DEAN JORDAN

My husband, a veteran, called a national cemetery to arrange for plots for the two of us.

"Is this for the active serviceman section or the inactive section?" asked the man on the other end of the line.

My flummoxed husband responded, "Lord! I hope they're all inactive."

—SALLY IDEN

Officers don't like to lose. Take, for example, one naval officer's write-up in the base newspaper of our unit's lunchtime softball game: "In a spirited end-of-season finale, the Khaki Special (officers/chiefs) team fought hard but finished the season in second place. Meanwhile, the enlisted personnel (the Blues) won their last game but finished next to last in the standings."

What he failed to mention about the season ... the two teams played only one game, against each other.

—J. KIRBY SPENCER

During ROTC, I reported to Fort Bragg in North Carolina for the summer training program. Trainees were handed piles of paperwork and ordered to fill in the blanks, beginning with our first and last names. Before I could start, I needed to clarify something with the sergeant in charge.

"My first name is John," I explained, "but I prefer to be called by my middle name, Fred."

He replied, "We'll be sure to keep that in mind ... John."

I took the hint. That summer, I learned to do everything the Army way.

—J. FRED RILEY

In basic training, our drill instructor made it clear that everything we recruits used belonged to her. For instance, she referred to our footlockers as "my trash," and the racks where we slept as "my racks." One time when we were all whispering in the bathroom while making "head calls," she surprised us by yelling, "Why do I hear voices in my head?"

—GCFL.NET

Reynolds

AN ACCIDENTAL VOLLEY IN THE COLD WAR

On the road to discovery, his experiment backfired

By Jonathan Walter

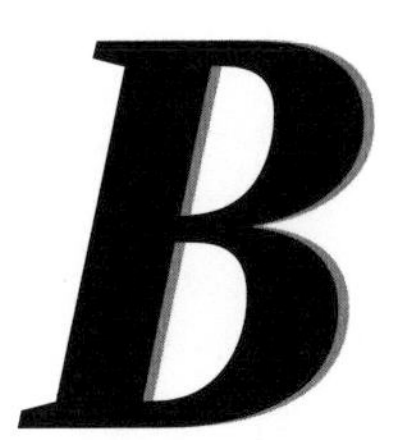

orn in Washington, D.C., less than a year before the Cuban missile crisis in 1962, I grew up when the fear of getting bombed by the Soviets was pervasive.

At age 3, my favorite place to sit in the car was on the hump in the front floor board so I could watch Dad work the pedals on our big Chrysler. (This was before mandatory child seats.)

That's where I was sitting one wintry day in February 1965. We were heading away from downtown on Rock Creek Parkway. Ahead of us was a car with four men wearing furry Cossack hats. Dad guessed they were from the Russian embassy and kept his distance. The last thing he wanted was to skid on a patch of ice and ram into them.

The Russians gave their turn signal as we approached Massachusetts Avenue. It's a long ramp, so we were driving parallel to them for several feet. Dad glanced at the Russians, who glanced back.

Meanwhile, I had become transfixed by Dad's keys dangling from the ignition. It suddenly dawned on me that they somehow made the car go. To test my theory, I reached through Dad's legs and turned the ignition key.

The Chrysler lurched wildly. Dad quickly realized the problem and shifted into neutral to restart, but not before the engine sucked in carbureted gasoline, which exploded inside the muffler in a string of bursts that sounded like machine gun fire.

All four furry hats vanished as the Russians ducked to save their lives from the crazy Americans firing on them. Their car left the road, spun 360 degrees on some ice and, amazingly, righted itself back onto the ramp. They sped away without a look back. And so did we. But now, against my will, I was on the seat.

During World War II, my Uncle Oliver was serving on a ship in the South Pacific when the crew ran low on food. All the sailors had left to eat was spaghetti—morning, noon and night for an entire month. At long last, they pulled into Melbourne, Australia, for supplies. There, the locals greeted them with a grand feast: all-you-can-eat spaghetti.

—LYNN LABONTE

Following a military reassignment, I moved into a home on a golf course called the Tournament Players Club (TPC). I phoned the electric company to set up service.

"My address is 5707 TPC Parkway," I told the rep.

"Was that DPC Parkway?" she asked.

"No, ma'am, it's ..."

"DBZ?"

"No, TPC—as in Tango Papa Charlie—Parkway."

"Oh, Tango Papa Charlie, right!"

Two weeks later, a letter from the utility arrived. It was addressed to me at "5707 Tango Papa Charlie Parkway."

—RONALD DOUGHERTY

My wife and I were watching a documentary about Navy SEALs going through POW training. Part of the exercise called for them to be placed in dog cages to simulate being captured.

'You know," I said to her, "when I was in the service, I went through similar training."

I expected her to be awed and impressed. Instead, she asked, "Do you think you can still fit in the cage?"

—JOHN UMHEY

During KP duty, my sergeant ordered me to prepare 100 gallons of soup for that night's dinner. When I told him I had no clue how to make soup, he handed me a cookbook and instructed, "Follow the directions carefully."

Not long after, I had a large kettle of soup simmering. The sergeant came in, grabbed a spoon and took a taste.

"This is great," he said. "Are you sure you followed the recipe?"

—NORMAN W. MIDDLETON

My uncle, a veteran of Normandy, always touted this famous saying: "Never worry about the bullet with your name on it. Watch out for the one addressed 'to whom it may concern.'"

— DICK HETLAND

Mistaken Identities

My first assignment as a second lieutenant was at NORAD headquarters. That first day, I encountered scads of high-ranking officers walking around and quickly found myself constantly saluting someone—a general here, a colonel there. It was only later when I learned that the last person in uniform I had saluted was a mailman.

—SKIP MCTIGHE

It was World War II—the front—and we were on high alert. Around midnight, I noticed movement behind a bush. Rather than fire a shot, I shouted out the first half of the password: "George!"

I waited for whoever it was to prove he was an American and reply with the countersign, "Marshall." Instead, silence.

"George!!" Again, no reply. I lifted up my rifle and gave it one last try: "George!!!"

An angry voice finally replied, "My name ain't George!"

—JAMES LIVESAY SR.

I was in a restaurant having lunch when I noticed four men dressed in camouflage uniforms seated nearby. I'm proud of the men and women who serve our country, so I walked over to the group and said, "I just want to thank you for your service, and it would be an honor to buy your lunch." One man put down his fork, looked up and said, "We appreciate that, ma'am; thank you. But we're not in the military. We're on a hunting trip."

—RENEE SETTLEMIRES

My son was stationed in Korea, and I couldn't stop thinking about him. So I baked a batch of his favorite cookies, packed them in a shoebox, wrapped the box and sent it halfway around the world. When he came home on leave, I asked him if he'd enjoyed the homemade cookies. He gave me a quizzical look and said, "Mom, you sent me your red shoes."

—JOAN SHELTON

When I spotted a Navy captain on the street, I saluted him and bellowed, "LST 395," which was the designation and number of the ship I served on during World War II.

The captain returned my salute and replied, "LMD 67."

"What's an LMD?" I asked him.

"Large Mahogany Desk."

—MICHAEL CIAVOLINO

We can thank soldiers and sailors for the words *umpteen, skedaddle* and *raunchy*. Here are other military slang terms that deserve widespread use.

- **Crumb catcher:** mouth
- **Five-sided puzzle palace:** the Pentagon
- **Flight suit insert:** pilot
- **Football bat:** an odd way of doing something
- **Fruit salad:** ribbons and medals worn on a uniform
- **Galloping dandruff:** lice
- **Geardo:** a soldier who obsesses about gear
- **Gofasters:** sneakers
- **Ink stick:** pen
- **Jesus slippers:** military-issued shower footwear
- **Left-handed monkey wrench:** a nonexistent item recruits are tricked into looking for
- **Oxygen thief:** someone who talks too much
- **Soup sandwich:** a situation that has gone horribly wrong
- **Voluntold:** forcibly volunteered for an assignment

—MILITARY.COM

Dad always bragged about the gunners on his ship. Once during target practice, an unmanned drone flew past an antiaircraft cruiser. The cruiser opened up, shells furiously flying all around the drone but not hitting it.

Then came Dad's ship's turn. The gunners' very first shot sent the drone into the water! Forty years later, Dad met the man responsible, and he told him how impressed he had been.

"Yeah, I got in a lot of trouble for that," the gunner said. "Turns out we were supposed to shoot around it, not hit it."

—PATRICK MCSHERRY

During an entrance interview with the Air National Guard, my niece was asked, "How long have you wanted to be a pilot?" She answered by recounting an adorable story of how she was videotaped by her mother at the age of 5 saying she wanted to grow up to be a "princess pilot." Her evaluator, unmoved, responded, "Princess interviews are next week, so we'll just focus on the pilot questions for now, OK?"

—MARK GARVEY

My nephew told his teacher that his mom is on parole. Actually, she's on patrol, serving in the National Guard.

—@CAI_LYFE

"Something tells me you haven't mastered the art of putting your rifle back together, soldier."

"It's the officer's foxhole."

Comedian Martha Raye was a great supporter of the military and made many trips to Vietnam to entertain the troops. She also liked to drink.

One day, I was told to report to my commanding officer, who ordered me to escort Ms. Raye. He then added confidentially, "We've already been through three escorts. You're the only one I can think of she won't be able to drink under the table."

—R.D.

I was sent to Japan by the Defense Language Institute Foreign Language Center to work with American linguists. One day, I contacted the operator and said that I wanted to call Monterey, California.

"How do you spell it?" she asked.

I said, "M as in Massachusetts, O as in Oregon, N as in Nevada ..."

"Wait, please," said the operator. "How do you spell Massachusetts?"

—YEFIM M. BRODD

Enlisted men: Never volunteer for any duty, no matter how enticing. At formation, a sergeant asked, "How many of you like music?" Three of us raised our hands.

"Good. You three report to the orderly room. You're going to move a piano into the day room."

—RICHARD T. FLOERSHEIMER

We were inspecting several lots of grenades. While everyone was concentrating on the task at hand, I held up a spare pin and asked, "Has anyone seen my grenade?"

—SMSGT. DAN POWELL FROM RALLYPOINT.COM

I run sophisticated weather programs on multimillion-dollar supercomputers at a Navy center for environmental predictions. That said, on the morning of one recent hurricane, my boss still beat me to reporting up-to-date details on the storm's status. Fascinated by his ability to summon reports so quickly, I asked him how to do it.

"Simple," he said. "Go turn on the television and watch the Weather Channel."

—GCFL.NET

While on maneuvers in the Mojave Desert, our convoy got lost, forcing our lieutenant to radio for help.

"Are you near any landmarks that might help us locate you?" the base operator asked.

"Yes," said the lieutenant. "We are directly under the moon."

—JESSE JOE WINGO

I GUESS WE'D BE LIVING IN A BORING, PERFECT WORLD IF EVERYBODY WISHED EVERYBODY ELSE WELL.

—JENNIFER ANISTON

The fascination of shooting as a sport depends almost wholly on whether you are at the right or wrong end of the gun.

—P.G. WODEHOUSE

You can no more win a war than you can win an earthquake.

—JEANNETTE RANKIN

It's possible to disagree with someone about the ethics of nonviolence without wanting to kick his face in.

—CHRISTOPHER HAMPTON

The only winner in the War of 1812 was Tchaikovsky.

—SOLOMON SHORT

The direct use of force is such a poor solution to any problem, it is generally employed only by small children and large nations.

—DAVID FRIEDMAN

The way to win an atomic war is to make sure it never starts.

—OMAR N. BRADLEY

I thoroughly disapprove of duels. If a man should challenge me, I would take him kindly and forgivingly by the hand and lead him to a quiet place and kill him.

—MARK TWAIN

Before a war military science seems a real science, like astronomy, but after a war it seems more like astrology.

—REBECCA WEST

IF YOU SHOOT AT MIMES, SHOULD YOU USE A SILENCER?

—STEVEN WRIGHT

GYM WAS "ATTACKED" BY WWII AIRCRAFT

A brief flight gave one youthful fighter "pilot" something to write about

By William Goetz

Shortly after the end of World War II, a surplus fighter airplane was given to my cousin's high school in Minnesota.

The Corsair F4U was flown to Minneapolis first. Then, with its wings folded, it was placed on a flatbed truck for the drive to Bemidji, then was unloaded in the school's parking lot.

After school, the kids flocked to the plane, climbing all over it. One bold lad even climbed into the cockpit.

Another young man jumped off the wing and grabbed one of the propellers. It began to turn slowly and lowered him to the ground. Soon, there was a line of boys, including my cousin, on the wing, waiting to jump on the blade and ease to the ground.

Meanwhile, the "pilot" continued to jiggle instruments and managed to turn on the ignition switch. The kids hanging on the prop blades were, of course, priming the engine.

It came to life with a frightful sputter. Most of the kids abandoned "ship," but the boy in the cockpit kept trying desperately to shut it off.

The plane began to move on its wheels toward the school building. With wings folded, it was never going to fly, but the plane was out of control.

It approached a brick wall of the gym and struck with a mighty *ka-whoomp,* killing the engine. One prop blade broke off, flew across the air and broke a window of a house across the street. Luckily, no one was injured.

The lad in the cockpit was shaken up. He'd hit his head on something and had to spend the night in the hospital, visited by all his "copilots."

He wrote up his experience for an English paper and received an A.

The title? "Thirty Seconds Over Bemidji High School."

ESSAY CREDITS

"Yard Sales: What a Way to Make a Buck!" by Will Stanton, *Reader's Digest*, April 2018. Originally published in *Reader's Digest*, May 1979

"Their Product Had a Short Shelf Life" by Adam Sibcy, *Reminisce*, April/May 2019

"Stranger Things" by Andy Simmons, *Reader's Digest*, September 2019

"Telepathy with ... My Dog?" by Patricia Pearson, *Reader's Digest* International Editions, June 2021

"Aim High" by Melody Durant, *Country Woman*, June/July 2021

"Parenting: To Coddle or Neglect?" by Richard Glover, *Reader's Digest* International Editions, January 2022

"Do Look Behind That Curtain" by Janet Ingram, *Reminisce*, October/November 2017

"A Cooked-Up Scheme Falls Flat" by Paul Kieffer, *Reminisce Extra*, September 2017

"Funny, You Don't Look like Daniel Craig" by Lenore Skenazy, *Reader's Digest*, August 2010

"A Virtuoso and Me" by Anne Semmes, *Reminisce*, August/September 2017

"Mad Science " by Andy Simmons, *Reader's Digest*, March 2010

"Worried Sick" by Billy Goldberg, M.D., and Mark Leyner, *Reader's Digest*, February 2011

"In Stitches" by Mariah Julio, *Country Woman*, February/March 2022

"I'm a Hero Behind the Wheel" by Richard Glover, *Reader's Digest* International Editions, July 2022

"A Coupe of a Different Color" by Martha Mahon, *Reminisce Extra*, November 2019

"An Open Letter to the Guys Who Kicked the Soccer Ball over the Fence and Asked Me to Toss It Back to Them, Thus Scarring Me for Life" by Jen Cordery, copyright © 2011 by Jen Cordery. McSweeneys.net (Jan. 3, 2012). *Reader's Digest*, April 2012

"Hockey Talk" by Sophie Kohn, *Reader's Digest Canada*, June 2022

"A Bird in the Hand" by Judy Pearce, *Reminisce Extra, March 2018*

"The Perfect Salon? A Barber Shop" by Patricia Pearson, *Reader's Digest* International Editions, November 2022

"Lost and Found" by DeLila Lumbardy, *Country Woman*, December/January 2022

"9 Really Practical Jokes" by the Javna Brothers, adapted from the book *Life Is a Joke*, copyright © 2017 by Gordon and John Javna. Reprinted with permission of Workman Publishing. *Reader's Digest*, April 2019

"Insect Interruption" by Karen Troncale, *Country Woman*, December/January 2021

"Alley Oops" by Camille Engeldt, *Reminisce*, October/November 2022

"An Accidental Volley in the Cold War" by Jonathan Walter, *Reminisce*, February/March 2018

"Gym Was 'Attacked' by WWII Aircraft" by William Goetz, *Reminisce Big Laughs*, 2006

CARTOON CREDITS

11 Leo Cullum

13, 53, 101, 118, 204 Dan Reynolds

18 Chris Wildt

39 Jimmy Craig/theycantalk.com

40 Mike Shiell

54 Conan de Vries

60 Peter Mueller

64 Ralph Hagen

74 Dave Blazek

80 Mark Anderson

83 Mike Shapiro

94, 108 Harley Schwadron

102, 177, 209 Jon Carter

124 Pat Byrnes

128 Kim Warp

137 P.C. Vey

144 Scott Masear

150, 201 Chris Weyant

158 Mick Stevens/*The New Yorker*

161 Dan McConnell

162 Robert Erskine

170 Evan Lian

185 Dave Carpenter

187 Bob Eckstein

196, 210 Bill Thomas

Cartoonstock:

23 Bob Mankoff

24, 167 John Grimes

32 Lonnie Millsap

27 Chris Wildt

37 Shannon Wheeler

45, 178 Leo Cullum

62 John Caldwell

84 Asher Perlman

121 Matthew Diffee

127 Frank Cotham

141 Joseph Farris

149 Ralph Hagen

188 Seth Fleishman